Getting REAL about Loving

"In *Loving the Me God Sees*, L... ... James to another level. She provides a roadmap to help you examine your heart to see if you are truly living as the person God created you to be. Her "down to earth," thought-provoking, and questioning approach makes you step back and think deeper. God knows the real you, but if your desire is to be *real* and *transparent* in your relationship with others, then this is the study for you."

>Debbie Morrison – mother to an adult son, wife to a tech geek

"*Loving the ME God Sees* proved to be a wonderful tool for self-discovery, emotional healing, community building, discipleship and spiritual growth... I learned to both forgive and begin to embrace myself. The concepts are deep, but the writing style is refreshingly uncomplicated... Goldfarb's vision of Christian women lovingly sharing each other's burdens, joys and journeys is timely and freeing."

>Mariana P. Dannelley, J.D. – College professor, writer, speaker, mentor, sister, mother, wife & friend.

"*Loving the ME God Sees* made me take a second look at what pride can be, yeah, it was a lot more than I thought. I love the fact that this Bible study brought a fresh perspective with practical application to my everyday challenges."

>Susan Bunce – Wife, mother, designer, business owner, and teacher.

"*Loving the ME God Sees* has encouraged me to use my *Faith-voice*, and has given me a greater confidence in my *Faith-walk*."

>Ginger Dispain – Worship Facilitator Team Leader and Daughter of God.

"*Loving the ME God Sees* was a refreshing study; I went through it twice. Each time God brought to my attention something new that He wanted to heal or change in my life. Linda has a gift for relating to others in a very real and authentic way. In turn, it invites others to freely share from their heart. I love the idea of being transparent and intentional in our relationships with others. That is something I now strive to accomplish. God blesses our relationships when we do the right thing!"

> Judy Dishong - Wife, mother of three grown children, grandmother of six teen-age grandchildren, and Ladies Sunday School teacher.

"As I experienced Linda's, *Loving the ME God Sees* study three times, my heart was opened, to identify the difference in the lies I had been telling myself, and the truth about who I am, found in God's word. Digging deeper into the book of James allowed His Truth to penetrate my heart as never before. If you're ready to experience God, family, and friendships at a deeper level, you must take this study."

> Teri Sundman – Wife, Mom, Nana, & mostly, lover of the Word.

"I have gone through *Loving the ME God Sees* Bible study twice, and God revealed different "aha's" about *me* each time. One thing I walked away with is, God loves me... not the way I see me, but through His eyes. I am a daughter of the King... just the way He made me."

> Cathey Edgington – wife, mom, grandmother, avid geocaching-gal, and Women's Ministry Financial and Administrative Director

"I originally took the *Loving the Me God Sees* Bible Study because honestly, as a young mother of 4 children, four and under; I needed a break! The title really caught my attention, as I've always struggled with self esteem, a character trait I don't want passed on to my children. During this study experience, we learned more about ourselves as we learned about God. I know now God intends for women to let down our walls, be real, and to build each other up. I definitely recommend this study to every woman."

> April Nel – twenty-something wife and mother of four under the age of five, lover of Jesus

Loving the ME God Sees

Linda Goldfarb

Foreword by Jennifer Kennedy Dean

Mid-Week H.U.G.s (His Unfailing Grace)
by Brenda Blanchard

Loving the ME God Sees
© 2014 by Linda Goldfarb
All rights reserved. First printing 2012
Printed in the United States of America

No part of this publication may be reproduced, stored in a retrieval system, or transmitted in any form or by any means – electronic, mechanical, photocopying, recording, or otherwise – without prior written permission of the author.

All Scripture quotations, unless otherwise indicated are taken from the Holy Bible, New King James Version NKJV copyright © 1982 by Thomas Nelson, Inc. Used by permission. All rights reserved.

Scripture quotations marked (NIV) are taken from the HOLY BIBLE, NEW INTERNATIONAL VERSION®. NIV®. Copyright ©1973,1978, 1984 by International Bible society. Used by permission of Zondervan. All rights reserved.

Scripture quotations marked (MSG) are taken from the Message by Eugene H. Peterson, Copyright ©1993, 1994, 1995, 1996, 2000. Used by permission of NavPress Publishing Group. All rights reserved.

Scripture quotations marked (NASB) are taken from the New American Standard Bible®, Copyright © 1960, 1962, 1963, 1968, 1971, 1972, 1973, 1975, 1977, 1995 by The Lockman Foundation. Used by permission.

Cover design by Thirty-Three Design
www.thirtythreedesign.com

ISBN 978-1-941733-04-2

EA Books, Inc.
eabooksonline.co

Those who helped me write transparently REAL...

Thank you to Cheri Cowell and her *patient* experts at EA Books for all the time and energy spent in production of this study.

When I heard the whisper to write this study, I struggled in my predisposed unworthiness. But God in His holiness would not allow me to sit in that pit of lies. One by one, He brought precious women into my writing journey. Each invested her time, distinct personality, spiritual maturity, and relational experience transparently into this study. Without them, umm, yeah...

Marianna Dannelley, Judy Dishong, Lisa Morris, Teri Sundman, Lorraine Swinney, and Jeanette Weatherly...thank you for your faithfulness to meet week after week unselfishly pouring into each other and into me as this study was written. I'm blessed beyond measure by the friendship God has given us.

Brenda Blanchard...you've been with me before the beginning as a spiritual mentor, prayer warrior and friend. You opened your home every week for our study time and your heart ever since as my sister in Christ. Your mid-week prayer H.U.G.s are a beautifully transparent addition to this study. Beyond His Unfailing Grace there are not words to describe what God has accomplished in my life through you.

My hubby, Sam, your willingness to allow me as much time as I needed to work on this passion-project absolutely empowered me to keep going. Knowing you had my back, as well as taking care of the daily functions of running our home, took the pressure off and helped me keep moving up to do all He asks of me.

I'm fully indebted to my Abba. You, O Lord, equip me daily through the Holy Spirit to live boldly, not defined by life's circumstances, but refined through them. You set my heart on fire for Your daughters, giving me a passion to share my deepest thoughts and experiences without fear. You alone deserve the glory and praise for lives changed and hearts opened through this study. Thank you for opening my heart to see how much You love me and for using this study to help my sisters experience Your love of them in the same way. May every work I write bring You honor and glory. Amen.

As we dig deeper into God's word,
His love for us, and *our* need for an intimate
relationship with him, is made more evident.
This study reveals the power and purpose of embracing
intimate-transparency in our relationship with God
and others.
When we, as His daughters, come together....rooted in
Truth, strengthened by sisterhood, and empowered by
the Holy Spirit, the enemy will have no
foothold in any season of our lives.
This freedom and hope is possible when we open
ourselves to experience relational transparency with
sisters of faith.
I pray this transparency will transform your life.

Linda

Contents

Foreword	11
Introduction	13
Overview	16
Session 1 – **Trials: Growing in Tough Times**	23

    Day 1 – The Bondservant
    Day 2 – Joy in the Midst of Trials
    Day 3 – Strength in the Midst of Trials
    Day 4 – Focus in the Midst of Trials
    Day 5 – Results in the Midst of Trials

Session 2 – **Temptation: Responding in Your Spiritual Nature**   37

    Day 1 – Endurance
    Day 2 – Desires
    Day 3 – Sin & Death
    Day 4 – Good Gifts
    Day 5 – God's Will

Session 3 – **Reflection: Showing Who You Serve**   51

    Day 1 – Servant of the World
    Day 2 – Servant of the Word
    Day 3 – Doer of the Word
    Day 4 – Useless in the World
    Day 5 – Useful in the World

Session 4 – **Impartiality: Seeing Through God's Eyes**   65

    Day 1 – An External View of Impartiality
    Day 2 – An Internal View of Impartiality
    Day 3 – Understanding the Royal law
    Day 4 – God's View of the Commandments
    Day 5 – Embracing the Law of Liberty

Session 5 – **Faith: Walking the Walk**   77
    Day 1 - Does My Faith Tell or Show?
    Day 2 - Is My Faith Passive or Active?
    Day 3 - Is My Faith Head Knowledge or Heart Belief?
    Day 4 - Am I Walking with Mature or Immature Faith?
    Day 5 - Can I Move From Religious Talk to an Everyday Faith-Walk?

Session 6 – **Words: Taming the Tongue**   89
    Day 1 - Listening 101
    Day 2 - Taking Charge
    Day 3 - Damage Control
    Day 4 - Taming the Tongue
    Day 5 - Producing Fruit

Session 7 – **Pride: Embracing Wisdom, Releasing Self**   105
    Day 1 - Spiritual Wisdom
    Day 2 - Earthly Pleasures
    Day 3 - Resist the Devil
    Day 4 - Humble Before God
    Day 5 - Judge Not

Session 8 – **Prosperity: Living in a Material World**   121
    Day 1 - Life is Good
    Day 2 - Thy Name is Misery
    Day 3 - Temptation to Accumulate
    Day 4 - Self-Imposed Grief
    Day 5 - Living Above Curses

Session 9 – **Perseverance: Rewarding Persistence**   139
    Day 1 - Establish Your Heart
    Day 2 - Do Not Grumble
    Day 3 - Consider the Prophets
    Day 4 - Accept the Lord's Mercy
    Day 5 - Hope in Christ

Session 10 – Action: Putting Feet to Your Faith   151
    Day 1 - Leaving Footprints of Integrity
    Day 2 - Casting Lifelines of Encouragement
    Day 3 - Leading By Example
    Day 4 - Walking in Confidence
    Day 5 - Mentoring With Love

Appendix   169
    One New Thought – Study Guides
    Resource Charts
        Chart 1 - I-Zone   **199**
        Chart 2 - Cross-References to James 4:11-17   **200**
        Chart 3 - Scripture References on Pride   **203**
        Chart 4 - I Am...My Identity in Christ   **208**
        Chart 5 - Terms of Theology   **209**

FOREWORD

Satan's ploy has not changed from the days of Eden. He started with a lie about how God sees us, and he has kept using it. It has worked for him since the first generation and will continue to work for him until the last generation. So, why reinvent the wheel? Keep using what works. Lie about the nature of God and about how the Father sees you. Keep shame alive. When we feel shame, we will naturally try to hide from God.

What robs that lie of its power over us? The truth. And it takes more than just knowing true doctrine at an intellectual level. It takes letting the Spirit of the Living God work it into our lives until it crowds out the lying narrative that forms or self-consciousness. It takes deliberate searching out truth, and then choosing truth over and over, even when the lie screams loudest and sounds most reasonable.

When we are fueled by shame, and Satan's lies have become our truth about who we are, then we find ourselves hiding not only from God, but from each other as well. It suits his agenda for us to be isolated from each other by pretenses—trying to cover our real selves with the fig leaf we harvested for ourselves. We panic when we feel the fig leaf slipping. "What if someone sees past my cover? They'll see that I'm naked and exposed and vulnerable and ugly."

We fear exposure more than we fear almost anything else. At the root of our anxieties and our anger and our selfishness is just fear of exposure, of being vulnerable. If Satan so strategically targets our shame and fear of exposure, don't you think it is because he knows that when we become transparent and vulnerable, we will find healing and wholeness? Satan has only one weapon in his arsenal: the lie. When he is deprived of that, then his ploy can't work.

In *Loving the Me God Sees*, Linda Goldfarb has mined a deep vein of truth. She unfolds the riches of the book of James and leads readers on a journey of transparency and truth. This is an experience—more than simply a study that will give you knowledge. It is aimed at transformation and healing, and it hits the mark.

I encourage you to approach this experience with anticipation. Fearless transparency on your part and the Spirit speaking truth into your life on His part, can't *not* transform you. You will grow both spiritually and relationally. Meet the *you* God sees. You will love her. She will astound you.

Jennifer Kennedy Dean
Executive Director, The Praying Life Foundation
Author of such books as *Live a Praying Life*,
The Power of Small, and *Altar'd*

INTRODUCTION

Welcome my sister to *Loving the ME God Sees*. Thank you for choosing to invest your precious time in this study on relational transparency. There are a few things about me I'd like to share with you as we begin; I'm the mother of four, grandmother of six, and wife of one – awesome guy named Sam. I've hosted several online radio and web-TV programs and encourage others with words wherever God sends me. I love spending time with my children and grandbabies, breathing in the freshness of the outdoors, sitting on my porch in the mornings sipping a steaming cup of coffee and writing to the glory of God. Okay wait… you may think my life sounds too good to be true, and I must admit, I often stop in awe of God and all He has done in my life, but it hasn't always been this way. You'll find out more about me as we journey together over the next few weeks… the sweet & stinky parts, for real, I have a lot of junk in my proverbial trunk.

I'd love to learn more about you as well, so please email me at linda@lindagoldfarb.com and let me know why you decided to go through this study and what your expectations are —we can learn about each other along the way.

So why did I write *Loving the ME God Sees*? As a speaker who writes, I didn't see me writing a Bible study at all, but as we know God's plans are not always our plans ☺. After two months of struggling with God —yes, I said struggling! Well, it might be best to start at the beginning… It began on a Monday morning in September 2009, with my usual routine of getting up early before the rest of the family, positioning myself on the couch in our sunroom, reading God's word, contemplating it's Truth and current relevance, and finally pondering how I was to apply it to my daily life. This one morning everything was going along as usual when I felt a specific prompting in my heart, "I want you to write a Bible study." Believe it or not, I actually looked around the room.

Once again an inaudible voice clearly said, "I want you to write a Bible study." I chuckled out loud, "You have got to be kidding! There is no way *I* could write a Bible study. *I* speak; *I* don't write, well, okay articles, and 'How-to Books' maybe, but not Bible studies. And besides, I'm not what anyone would consider a Bible scholar."

I breathed in a deep sigh and quietly justified my feelings, "I think there's been a mistake." With that, I went on about my day refusing to acknowledge a "whisper" as Bill Hybels calls it, from my Father. . . the struggle was on.

Over the course of two months, God's *whisper* remained a constant companion during my quiet time as did my refusal to consider it. Finally on a Friday morning early in November 2009, I'd had enough. His whisper was not going away, "Fine, if You really want me to write this study, I need to know it's of You and not just a whim I'm dreaming up. So… today I am claiming the wisdom You say You want to give me according to James 1:5 and I am believing that this day You will make it clear if I am to begin writing a Bible study." With that, I closed my Bible and walked into the rest of my day.

Late that afternoon, I was meeting with some friends of mine from church. When I arrived at our get together, Brenda Blanchard (a dear friend and mighty prayer warrior) walked up to me in her usual sensitive caring way and said, "Linda, you know I pray for you everyday, right? Well, this morning during my quiet time, God said you were writing a Bible study. What's it about?"

After a moment of standing there dazed by her pronouncement, I looked up towards the sky, looked back at Brenda and sputtered, "What did you say?" We laughed together in amazement when I explained the last couple months and my refusal to obey God and His persistence to not let me go about business as usual. The rest as they say is. . . this story of *Loving the ME God Sees*. Is God good or what?

God pulled no punches in letting me know what I was to do. He also provided a core group of women to go through the writing process with me, literally… He picked them out, gave me the names and told many of them ahead of time they were going to be doing something with me. Beginning in January 2010, over the course of thirteen weeks, the journey you are about to embark on spilled forth in my writing, I am honored to be here with you.

Loving the ME God Sees has been refined as a 10-week introspective and interactive small group study that helps women in every stage of life to understand *their love-letter from God*, found in the book of James. This study invites a unique transformation to occur in each woman's life at a spiritually deep and relationally transparent level without fear of being overwhelmed, intimidated or discouraged in her relationship with God, family, and friends. This is an area I have struggled with most of my life. . . trusting God enough to let the real me show up. During our time together, I will share what God has done in my life to peel away many of the barriers that held me back from getting real and finally enjoying God and life in an intimate and powerful way. What God has done and continues to do in my life He can and will do in yours.

Experiencing this deeper understanding of who we are in God's eyes, will peel back your *relational onion*, removing layers of false narratives so many of us believe about ourselves. False narratives will be replaced with biblically sound truths about God's love and plan for us as His daughters. This fresh perspective will open your spiritual eyes to the transparent relationships you are meant to experience with your Lord, loved ones and friends right now in the kingdom of God.

As you go through the scriptures each week, you will be encouraged to consider the truth you are reading, its relevance today, and it's application to your life. These three simple thought processes will be a core element in your weekly study, and if nothing else, you will walk away from this study able to take any scripture and put it into fruitful action.

With God's grace and your willingness to listen to *His* whispers, I call that "getting skinny with the Spirit," *Loving the ME God Sees* could be the catalyst you use to embrace life with a renewed vigor, determined to breathe in every moment of every day with a redirected outlook powered by *The Power Source* that never fails. The same Power that raised Jesus from the dead is available to every believer in Christ. Through this study we will focus on His power and possibilities for your life so you will love yourself as He loves you.

Hugs in Him. . . Linda

OVERVIEW

Name: _____

Small Group Leader(s)_____

_____

What is Introspective Study?

Introspective study is a meditative, reflective, and personal look into ourselves. . . getting real from the inside out.

Your dedication to the weekly study questions will serve to provide you a deeper understanding of where you are at this season in your life spiritually, physically and relationally. How the scriptures speak directly to you may be unique from your small group sisters based on your current season, so sharing your thoughts will be encouraged. This study should move you into a deeper relationship with Christ on a very real level.

You have a five-day study guide for the following week's small group meeting, so you will be able to choose any five days out of seven to complete your weekly entries and sharing's. You'll notice I didn't say weekly "work." The reason is simple. . .I have found when I sit a little longer at the table of our Heavenly Father it becomes a time of refreshment for me, not work. . . and I believe you will receive the same. You will notice the length of the passages for each day are short, this gives you time to dig a little deeper. Please have your Bible and dictionary handy as you go through the daily readings. Multiple translations are good as well. Okay, wait, don't get alarmed. . . if digging deeper isn't your style, then simply do as much as you can.

In addition to your entries and sharings, you will be asked to look up some scripture (References provided) but for those of you who really want to *Dig Deeper* you will look for the Double D "DD" options each week, then jot down your thoughts for small group discussion. This is optional, but highly recommended for the study to be life changing.

As a special bonus, I'm including the prayers and encouragement my good friend and Bible teacher, Brenda Blanchard, emailed to our small groups each week during LMGS's first official teaching. I speak a lot on the power of hugs, I call them relational food. In as much as relational hugs are experienced in the physical, spiritual H.U.G.s (**H**is **U**nfailing **G**race is sufficient) are felt through prayer, encouragement, and God's Word. Therefore, we are calling Brenda's mid-week offerings, H.U.G.s. I pray you are blessed by her anointed writing. You can find out more about Brenda at www.BrendaBlanchard.com.

Loving The ME God Sees' weekly scriptures are from the New King James Version Bible. You'll be asked what Bible translation you use and why you use that particular translation to help your sisters broaden their scope on what is available in the marketplace. Then you are able to share with your small group different words you find in the scripture each week and why they stand out to you. We've found this to be an enlightening time for all the groups.

A bit of inductive study is included free of charge because we need to *know what we know*—and to find out things for ourselves—you will be prompted to mark up your Bible as well, but this is an option not a mandate. My purpose for this is to get you comfortable with God's word as a natural part of your daily life; you may want to write notes in the margins for your children, spouse, friends, grandchildren or as a reminder of "who" needs to hear this. Thus, God's word becomes your daily bread. . . nourishment for your soul.

> "One of the great things about sisters in Christ is they help to keep the real deal in front of me by holding me accountable to my spiritual walk."
>
> Laurie Zieber - Inspirer of women, owner of Sugar Britches at The Mountain in Canton TX, and my sweet friend.

Loving the ME God Sees offers you something every woman wants… the opportunity to be real without fear of judgment or ridicule. . . Hence relational transparency.

What is Relational Transparency?

This study will be one of transparency without judgment. . . an opportunity to grow in ways we have never experienced before. Like the Redwoods of California, you and your small group members will become connected at the roots, as sisters in Christ and warriors for His kingdom. Holding each other up when the storms of life come, rejoicing in the victories and helping each other to grow to heights unfathomable to the world, as Daughters of the King.

I want you to consider your time together and your study location a safety-zone. This is one place you and your sisters can tell-it-like-it-is without fear of rejection. There will be accountability and definite truth-telling but anything shared in small group is to remain confidential. So let's keep the real-deal out there in front. One of the things we found going through our original meetings, is God seemed to prompt one person to really share and open up each week. We believe it may happen that same way in your small group. So as you are led, allow the Holy Spirit to carry your words, needs, and concerns to your sisters.

One way to do this is to be open with your thoughts, as prompted by the Holy Spirit, when you share during our small-group time. During the next 10 weeks, you will discover things about yourself you may never have understood before. You are asked to fully rely on God as your guide and your small group sisters as your safety net of sorts. You are not here to counsel each other, but to be who you are created to be. . . caring sisters, supernaturally enabled by the Holy Spirit to connect with each other at a deeper-than-usual level.

Name Your Season

"To everything there is a season, and a time to every purpose under the heaven: A time to be born, and a time to die; a time to plant, and a time to pluck up that which is planted; A time to kill, and a time to heal; a time to break down, and a time to build up; A time to weep, and a time to laugh; a time to mourn, and a time to dance; A time to cast away stones, and a time to gather stones together; a time to embrace, and a time to refrain from embracing; A time to get, and a time to lose; a time to keep, and a time to cast away; A time to rend, and a time to sew; a time to keep silence, and a time to speak; A time to love, and a time to hate; a time of war, and a time of peace" (Ecclesiastes 3:1-8 NKJV).

It's apparent from this scripture, seasons of our lives are not restricted to our chronological age, As we read in Ecclesiastes, there is a season for everything... what season are you living right now. . . one of relational famine, financial feast, or physical challenges? A season of aging parents. . . where you are the caregiver. . . a season of loss, mourning a loved one? Or a season of joy because of a new job or positive news that has come into your life. It's important to know what season you are in because it brings reality into our midst. . . knocking down the walls of pretence thus creating a common ground among future best friends. If you're not sure of your season, list some of the things you are experiencing in your life right now.

My Season:

We are each unique as daughters of the Most High and some of us are going through tougher seasons than others, yet if we continue reading in Ecclesiastes 3:14 we find a message of reassurance that no matter our season, God is in control. As His daughters we can wrap our hands around this to give us hope... *"I know that, whatsoever God doeth, it shall be forever: nothing can be put to it, nor any thing taken from it: and God doeth it, that men should fear before him."* This is not a fear of dread; it's a fear of reverence... recognizing *Who* God is and living a life that shows it.

How does this make you feel?

Now we have a grasp on our season, let's go a bit deeper and examine our faith-walk. Remember, no judgment here, just getting real with ourselves and God.

Measuring Your Faith-Walk:

"I waited patiently for the LORD; And He inclined to me, And heard my cry. He also brought me up out of a horrible pit, Out of the miry clay, And set my feet upon a rock, And established my steps. He has put a new song in my mouth— Praise to our God; Many will see it and fear, And will trust in the LORD" (Psalm 40:1-3 NKJV).

Rate these statements truthfully for your current season. (For your eyes only)

Empty...1...2...3...4...5...6...7...8...9...Full

1. I wait *patiently* for the Lord in the following areas:

Family _____
Spouse _____
Work _____
Strangers _____
Self _____

2. I cry out to my Abba on a *regular* basis. (In joy, sadness, praise, adoration, etc.) ___

3. I experience the Arms-of-God lifting me out of trials *consistently*. (In all things) ___

4. I am planted *firmly* on the rock of faith. (No worry, anxiety, doubt, fear) ___

5. The *Holy Spirit* establishes my steps. (Everything is done His way not mine) ___

6. I sing out a *new song* of praise to God daily. (Fresh-excitement, full of wonder and awe) ___

7. My Faith-Walk *inspires others* to trust the Lord. ___

This is just a starting place so you can witness the power of God working in your life during our time together in this study.

Who is James?

James, the half-brother of Jesus, most likely wrote the book of James. See scripture references below to support this. Look them up and make notes on what you learn.

Mark 6:2-3

1 Cor. 15-7

Acts 15:6-21

Acts 21:17-18

Matthew 13:55

Galatians 1:19

Evidence of the life of James can also be found outside of the Bible, from the historian Josephus. In *Antiquities*[1], book 20 chapter 9, he mentions James the brother of Jesus and Annas the High priest.
It's important to *know what we know* and can *back it up with scripture*. . . this strengthens our faith-walk.

Points to Ponder... for Session 1

1. Who am I as a child of God?

2. How do I find joy in the midst of trials?

3. How do I find strength in the midst of trials?

4. Where should I focus in the midst of trials?

5. What results can I expect in the midst of trials?

Session 1: Growing in Tough Times

"And the true realism, always and everywhere, is…to find out where joy resides, and give it a voice far beyond singing. For to miss the joy is to miss all."
Robert Louis Stevenson

Session 1: Growing in Tough Times

Weekly Reading: James 1:1–11 NKJV *"James, a bondservant of God and of the Lord Jesus Christ, to the twelve tribes which are scattered abroad: Greetings. My brethren, count it all joy when you fall into various trials, knowing that the testing of your faith produces patience. But let patience have its perfect work, that you may be perfect and complete, lacking nothing. If any of you lacks wisdom, let him ask of God, who gives to all liberally and without reproach, and it will be given to him. But let him ask in faith, with no doubting, for he who doubts is like a wave of the sea driven and tossed by the wind. For let not that man suppose that he will receive anything from the Lord; he is a double-minded man, unstable in all his ways. Let the lowly brother glory in his exaltation but the rich in his humiliation, because as a flower of the field he will pass away. For no sooner has the sun risen with a burning heat than it withers the grass; its flower falls, and its beautiful appearance perishes. So the rich man also will fade away in his pursuits."*

Take a minute and read through this passage of scripture, if you use a different translation, underline where the two have different words and phrases of significance. Do any of the differences stand out to you? Why?

Session 1: Day 1 – The Bondservant
James 1:1
"James, a bondservant of God and of the Lord Jesus Christ, to the twelve tribes which are scattered abroad: Greetings."

1. During the introduction, you heard evidence of James relationship to Jesus. (1 Cor. 15-7, Acts 15:6-21, Acts 21:17-18, Matthew 13:55, Gal. 1:18-19) He knew Jesus his whole life, but didn't begin his ministry, as Pastor of the *Church of Jerusalem*, until after Christ's resurrection. Why do you think it took him so long?

2. Considering James' delay in stepping out in faith into his ministry, how does this speak to your walk with the Lord?

During *The Year of Jubilee* (Leviticus 25:8-17, 19-55) masters were required to forgive the debt of slaves who were considered *brethren* and to allow them safe journey back to their homes. But some chose to stay with their masters, these were considered bondservants. James calls himself a *bondservant* of God and of the Lord Jesus Christ.

The bondservant is a slave who chose to stay under the master's care, because life with the master was better than life out in the world. It is said that if the master agreed, the freed slave would willingly allow the master to pierce his earlobe with an awl, removing a huge hunk of skin so everyone would know he was a free-bondservant. As the bondservant walked through the market place, people would remark, "Wow, his master must really be good for him to want to stay!"

> *Bondservant* (Greek Doulos): devoted to another to the disregard of one's own interests.

3. Do you see yourself as a bondservant of Christ? If so, how do others see the *goodness* of your master in you? Do you offer outward signs of who you serve? If not, why?

4. Who is James writing to in this epistle? Why is this relevant to us today?

As you go about today. . . take note of opportunities God presents for you to show the world who He is in your life. Before you begin your lesson for tomorrow come back here and answer this. Did you find it easy or difficult to release the moment to God, giving Him the utmost honor? Why or why not?

Daily Prayer: *I praise You oh Lord for this insight into James. Help me understand who I am in You and how You can work through me for Your glory. Guide me this week so others will see Your goodness in me in ways they never have before. Ignite my servant's heart with a desire to reflect You in all I do. Amen*

Thoughts:

Session 1: Day 2 – Joy in the Midst of Trials
James 1:24
"My brethren, count it all joy when you fall into various trials, knowing that the testing of your faith produces patience. But let patience have its perfect work, that you may be perfect and complete, lacking nothing."

1. What does *joy* mean to you?

2. Why do you think James begins this teaching on faith with a focus on joy?

3. What trials have you experienced in the last twelve months?

4. Do you find it easy to ". . . count it all joy when you fall into… trials?"

    In January of 2008 I attended a spiritual retreat in a working Monastery near Oceanside, CA. and sat under the teaching of William Gaultiere (Bill). One morning Bill shared how the seed-cones of the giant Redwood trees, roughly the size of an extra large pecan, had to be exposed to fire before they could germinate and grow to their potential height of 360 feet. He compared it to our Christian walk; until we experience fire (trials); we can never grow to God's potential for our lives.
    I was fascinated with Bill's story and began my own research into the comparison of Redwood trees and our faith-walk. I discovered that their name *Sequoia Sempervirens* means *forever living*. Even though they are exposed to fire several times a year, it has little damaging effect on mature trees. One more thing I found fascinating, though some Redwoods grow over 360 feet tall, they have very shallow roots and can be easily toppled by strong winds and fierce weather. Very seldom is a Redwood standing alone, most are in groves where the roots from one

tree comingles with others around it giving all the trees a stronger support system than they could achieve on their own.

    Is this not like us? As children of the King we *live forever*. When mature Christians come under attack we withstand it by the power of the Holy Spirit in us. Finally left on our own, we tend to falter when the winds of life blow hard. However, if together, rooted at the deepest level, we can withstand whatever this world can throw at us. That's one reason I knew this study needed to be written, I believe we need to be rooted deeply with one another and that it can only happen when we come together... united as super-natural sisters in Christ. I pray this little aside will heighten your desire to connect at root-level with the other sisters in your small group.

5. What is your immediate reaction when you experience trials? Who or what do you lean on? Why? [Honesty is really needed here for us to minister to each other. . . say what you really do. . . hide away, turn to food, act rebellious, share your woes with everyone, go to one person. . .]

6. How do you feel after you turn to your first response?

7. When you read " . . . knowing that the testing of your faith produces patience." Do you really *know* that? Is *knowing* the same as believing? Why or why not?

8. What do you think James meant by "let patience have its perfect work, that you may be perfect and complete, lacking nothing"?

9. Share a time when the testing of your faith resulted in patience. How did it impact your spiritual life?

As you go about today ask the Lord to bring to your memory the joy of one trial from your past. Ponder it and write down any thoughts that come to you.

Daily Prayer: *Father, as I step out on the journey of Loving the ME God Sees, protect me from the twinges of remorse, fear, and anxiety from my past. Keep my focus on You and help me to dig deeper into myself to see more of You there. Amen.*

Here is your mid-week H.U.G. (His **U**nfailing **G**race**) from Brenda...**

I pray you are feeling blessed by the Lord this week. Write down some of your blessings below; we have so many:

Then, when you're feeling low, look at your list, and a big smile will cross your lips.

I was thinking today how much I postpone crucifying the flesh, even when the sin is right before me. Do you do that, too? Acts 24:24-25 says, "*Several days after Felix came with his wife Drusilla, who was a Jewess. He sent for Paul and listened to him as he spoke about faith in Christ Jesus. As Paul discoursed on righteousness, self-control, and the judgment to come, Felix was afraid and said, 'That's enough for now! When I find it convenient, I will send for you.'*"

It's no fun to deny the flesh its pleasures. But, I have found that it's always good for me to live in the Spirit. In order to do that, I have to recognize my sin and repent. The Lord is so good as He shows me only one at a time, so we can tackle it together. He is merciful and patient with me, but He hates the sin and wants me to deny its power in my life. When I finally quit postponing looking at the action, emotion, etc. as sin, I can through Christ do something about it. So, I have learned God doesn't give up on making me more like His Son, so I might as well quit postponing the destruction of whatever sin He lays before me. I have a long way to go, but I'm a child of the King and He never leaves me nor forsakes me. His love gives me the desire to please Him, and if that mean letting go, then so be it. Praise be to God!

Dear Father,

I come to you this morning full of love for you. Thank you for your Son, my Savior and Lord, Jesus, and also for the gift of your indwelling Holy Spirit. I ask for your hand to be on all the women in Linda's Bible study. I ask for favor for them in all that they are facing. Lord, we know nothing is too big for you to handle. We also ask that the women will lay down any sins that you have been dealing with them about, so that you can give them all the fullness of life you have planned for them. You have so much that you want to give them. We ask for your gentle caress to heal their hearts and minds of things they won't let go of and to trust that you can reconcile them to you and to others. You are worthy of all praise and honor and glory. The ladies have so many needs: dealing with illness, cancer, upcoming surgeries, attacks from the evil one, jobs, searching for homes, seeking wisdom, protection from false beliefs, salvation for loved ones, finances, time to be alone with you, being obedient to your ministry call. Lord, we know you are faithful and righteous and your will is supreme. We lift all their needs to you and ask for your divine hand to touch each request in such a way that these women know it is from you. We love you and know we can do nothing apart from you.

In Jesus' name, Amen

Session 1: Day 3 – Strength in the Midst of Trials
James 1:5
"If any of you lacks wisdom, let him ask of God, who gives to all liberally and without reproach, and it will be given to him."

1. When you are in the midst of a trial, what challenges you the most? When are you the weakest?

2. Do you consider yourself a woman who thrives when challenged or one who avoids a challenge at all costs? How has your response worked for you in this past year?

3. Define Wisdom:

4. We are told in today's reading to ask God to give us wisdom. Is this something you do on a regular basis or only during special times? Explain

5. Who is the *him* James refers to here when he writes, " . . . let him ask of God, who gives to all liberally and without reproach, and it will be given to him." Explain your answer.

6. Does this mean anything we ask from God, He will give us because He has so much to give?

7. What's the difference between knowledge and wisdom? How has God's wisdom strengthened you?

As you go about your day, list the ways you gained wisdom, at home, work, or out and about.

How can you be sure the wisdom came from God?

Daily Prayer: *Abba, I ask you to bring clarity to my mind concerning wisdom. Help me to recognize the work of Your hand in my life so I may be equally aware of the lies of this world. I do not want to be deceived; I desire to be empowered by You to walk strong in my faith. Amen.*

Thoughts:

Session 1: Day 4 – Focus in the Midst of Trials
James 1:6-8

"But let him ask in faith, with no doubting, for he who doubts is like a wave of the sea driven and tossed by the wind. For let not that man suppose that he will receive anything from the Lord; he is a double-minded man, unstable in all his ways."

1. Do you ever find yourself in the same boat as the Apostle Thomas (John 20:24-29), doubting the truth until you have tangible proof? How does today's reading, which is a continuation of yesterday's discussion on asking for wisdom, say we are to approach the Lord? Is this easy for you or not? Explain.

2. What does, ". . . let him ask in faith. . . " mean?

3. How can we live a doubt-free existence? Is it really possible?

4. James is really making a pivotal point here for believers. We are not to assume God will give us wisdom if we are not willing to walk in faith believing in the outcome. Does this mean we are to fake it until we make it?

5. Could this verse be suggesting we (believers) may be too full of ourselves, unwilling to ask God for help <u>until</u> we exhaust all our options? We walk around with one face and go home with another?

6. Why does God want us to ask for wisdom?

7. What is more difficult for you, to ask for wisdom on behalf of others or for your own sake? Why?

> *Double-minded*: Acting one way while feeling very differently, especially when this involves hypocrisy or deceit.

As you go about your day focus on God's presence in your activities and thank Him for what you observe. Be ready to share with the group.

Daily Prayer: *Praise You my Prince of Peace, King of Kings and Lord of Lords. Help me to doubt less and less, and to believe more and more. Create in me the desire to step out on the unseen bridge of Your mercy and grace on a daily basis so my path-of-faith becomes familiar to my heart. Amen.*

Session 1: Day 5 – Results in the Midst of Trials
James 1:9-11

"Let the lowly brother glory in his exaltation but the rich in his humiliation, because as a flower of the field he will pass away. For no sooner has the sun risen with a burning heat than it withers the grass; its flower falls, and its beautiful appearance perishes. So the rich man also will fade away in his pursuits."

> *Exaltation*: a feeling of intense or excessive happiness or exhilaration.

1. Who is the *lowly brother* mentioned in this passage?

2. Why would the *rich* find glory in his humiliation? What does that mean?

3. The rich person is compared to a flower. Why did James choose that comparison?

4. Is wealth what separates the two believers mentioned in these verses? Explain your answer:

5. What does this passage convey to you about the pursuit of happiness and success?

6. Our society places a big emphasis on happiness and the mighty dollar. How would you explain these verses to a non-believer in a way that is inviting yet does not step off-center when it comes to truth?

As you go about your day ask yourself if you might be seen as one who is concerned about the things of this world so much so that the joy in your life is diminished. Write down what you observe.

Daily Prayer: *Dear God, precious Father… I do not want to wither under the scorching heat of this world; I desire the positive results of a faith-full life. Open my eyes to Your will for my life. Turn my thoughts to You oh God in ways that I have never experienced before. I trust You Lord with all my heart. Help me to find Your grace sufficient.* Amen.

Session 2: Temptation: Responding in Your Spiritual Nature

"No man knows how bad he is till he has tried very hard to be good."
C.S. Lewis

Session 2: Temptation: Responding in Your Spiritual Nature

Weekly Reading: James 1:12-18 NKJV *"Blessed is the man who endures temptation; for when he has been approved, he will receive the crown of life which the Lord has promised to those who love Him. Let no one say when he is tempted, 'I am tempted by God'; for God cannot be tempted by evil, nor does He Himself tempt anyone. But each one is tempted when he is drawn away by his own desires and enticed. Then, when desire has conceived, it gives birth to sin; and sin, when it is full-grown, brings forth death. Do not be deceived, my beloved brethren. Every good gift and every perfect gift is from above, and comes down from the Father of lights, with whom there is no variation or shadow of turning. Of His own will He brought us forth by the word of truth, that we might be a kind of first fruits of His creatures."*

Take a minute and read through this passage of scripture. If you use a different translation, underline where the two have different words and phrases of significance. Do any of the differences stand out to you? Why?

☺**Note from Linda:** This study is very introspective. God wants us to be willing to go deeper, not only in His word but into ourselves as well, in order to recognize how powerful and loving He truly is. As you go through this week, ask the Holy Spirit to open your heart to transparent answers.

Session 2: Day 1 – Temptation: Endurance
James 1:12

"Blessed is the man who endures temptation; for when he has been approved, he will receive the crown of life which the Lord has promised to those who love Him."

Optional - Place a gold triangle on the words **Lord** and **Him** to designate the holiness of God. As we go through this week's study, anytime you see a reference to God (He, Himself, His) mark it with a gold triangle.

1. What does *blessed* mean to you? Give some examples:

2. Which one definition below, best describes *endure* in this season of your life? (Underline your choice)

- To experience exertion, pain, or hardship without giving up
- To tolerate or accept somebody or something that is extremely disagreeable
- To last or survive over a period of time, especially when faced with difficulties

Why does the definition you picked resonate with you right now?

Temptation:
[1] *A desire or craving for something, especially something considered wrong.*
[2] *The incitement of desire or craving in somebody.*

---

3. List the temptations you are aware of in your life currently:

4. Looking back at the definition you chose for *endure* and the temptations you listed, how successful do you think you will be to endure them in the next year? Write out next to each temptation a number from 0 – 5. Zero is considered "unsuccessful" and five is "a done deal". Now write why you will or will not succeed.

5. Look up *crown-of-righteousness* (life), how does it make you feel knowing you are promised this? 2 Timothy 4:8

6. James uses the word *approved* in this verse. What does approved mean to you?

7. What does it mean to *love* God?

As you go about today ask the Holy Spirit to bring to your mind areas of temptation you have endured for His good. Praise Him for those memories.

Daily Prayer: *Heavenly Father, my heart desires to feel worthy of the crown of life you have promised me. Help me to be aware of the temptations in my life and give me the endurance to withstand them. Amen*

What thoughts came to mind as you worked on today's lesson? Be prepared to share:

Session 2: Day 2 – Temptation: Desires
James 1:13-14

"Let no one say when he is tempted, 'I am tempted by God'; for God cannot be tempted by evil, nor does He Himself tempt anyone. But each one is tempted when he is drawn away by his own desires and enticed."

1. James tells us straight out that God does not *tempt* us. Where does temptation come from? How does this make you feel?

2. Find evidence to support the author's claims that God cannot be tempted by evil (He is holy). Exodus 3:5; Isaiah 48:17; Leviticus 19:2 are just a few. Write your findings here:

3. When you give into temptation, based on your desires, is it a reaction (off the top of your head) or a response (after you think on it for a while)? Give an explanation for your choice:

    When Sam and I were about a year and a half into our marriage, we found ourselves on a very rough road. Though I wasn't contemplating divorce, I had several friends and a family member telling me, "You don't deserve this. You deserve to be happy and need to feel loved. Maybe you should get a divorce."
    I must admit, everything they said rang true in my ears. I so desired to be happy and to feel loved. After all, I had already spent ten years in a marriage that resulted in heartache and pain; did I really want to go through that again? When I was at my lowest point I would call one of my friends to hear their confirmation of my feelings. . . "I don't deserve this."
    I can tell you right now, God really was holding on tight to my spiritual hand during this time and He caused a check in my spirit about a word I kept hearing; *Deserve*. . . There may be many things I desire in life because it might make me happy, but very few things I deserve because I'm so *good*. Almost instantly I recognized what I had been doing. I had bought into everything my friends-of-good-intentions had offered instead of going to God. I praise Him for not letting go of me when I was struggling so hard to get away. August 2013 Sam and I

celebrated twenty-seven years of marriage. We are blessed with so many stories about God's grace and favor. Be aware that the *good* intentions of others may not fit into God's *best plan* for us.

4. Define the word *entice* what word does your translation use in its place?

5. When I hear the word entice, it makes my skin crawl, it just seems evil. James tells us we are tempted when we are drawn away by our desires and *enticed*. How are you enticed? Is there a "someone" (peer, colleague, friend, etc) or a "something" (TV, radio, internet, magazines, etc) that draws you into temptation? (This is not meant to be a moment of justification, just a time of deeper awareness). List them here:

Would you be willing to share this with your group. . . pray about it?

As you go about today be alert to life around you and *name* temptation as it comes into your path. This will really tick off the evil one.

Daily Prayer: *Abba, Daddy. . . open my eyes to be alert to "temptation" set in place around me. Give me wisdom to recognize the many shapes it comes in and to be quick to name it and disclaim it.* Amen.

Here is your mid-week H.U.G. (His **U**nfailing **G**race**) from Brenda...**

Hi Sweet Saints,
    I pray your week is one where you walk faith-full-y with Jesus! There are times when I feel helpless--as though there is nothing more I can do. My faith seems small in comparison to others. My resources are limited. I can only look up and hope against all hope that God will have mercy on me. And, He does. He always does. I am convinced again that "with God, all things are possible." He is faithful. He is Abba, Father, and I am His child.

"In the future when I'm in need," I tell myself, "I will begin with prayer." Why do I keep trying on my own? Why do I fail to trust in my Maker? Why do I worry, fret, and stew over circumstances, relationships, finances, health. . . ? I have found my best efforts are futile time after time. Prayer should be my first line of defense. I guess that's why John Wesley said, "Prayer is where the action is." Lord, let me start at the action point from now on.

Abba, Father,
Thank You for this beautiful day and for Your unconditional love for us. Thank You for Your forgiving heart, for the grace You give us time after time. Help us to seek You with all our hearts, souls, and minds. In that, we will find great strength and peace. Let us know that You have all answers, and let us begin searching for our answers through You first. Keep our minds free from worry and thoughts that are not pleasing to You. Remind us that You know our every need, and that You can heal all relationships. Encourage us to be witnesses. Strengthen our marriages, our friendships, our finances. Open doors for employment and use us in our work places to show Christ through our attitudes and good work ethics. We know, also, Lord, that you heal "all diseases and afflictions" and that no illness is out of Your realm of healing. Nothing is incurable to You, so we plead the blood of Jesus over those needing a healing in their bodies. Thank You that You know our every move, and that in our travels, You are with us, keeping us safe, and sending Your angels before us. We praise You for the answered prayers and the ones You are answering even as we pray this prayer. You are Jehovah El Shaddai, and You meet our every need. In Jesus' precious Name, we pray in agreement. Amen.

Session 2: Day 3 – Temptation: Sin & Death
James 1:15-16
"Then, when desire has conceived, it gives birth to sin; and sin, when it is full-grown, brings forth death. Do not be deceived, my beloved brethren."

1. Satan works in our weaknesses (negative thinking, poor attitudes, unforgiveness, etc.). What weaknesses are you living with today?

2. We know we are born into a sinful nature because of the *fall* of Adam and Eve (Romans 3:23). We also know the wages for sin is death (Romans 6:23) but... in the same verse of Romans we are promised eternal life as a gift from God, in the life of Jesus Christ. So... how do we then, as believers, experience *death* as mentioned in this passage because of full-grown sin? What do you think? (**DD** – find scripture to support your thoughts)

3. *"Do not be deceived, my beloved brethren."* Our desires can deceive us. Desires begin in the mind... as we think. What does God's word tell us about how we are to think? (Research on your own or look up Psalm 19:14; Romans 1:28; 8:6-7; Matthew 22:37)

Consider the comparison of our sinful and spiritual nature; be prepared to give your thoughts.

SINFUL NATURE	**SPIRITUAL NATURE**
Focuses on the things of the flesh (Rom. 8:5)	Focuses on the things of the Spirit (Rom. 8:5)
Is death (Rom. 8:6)	**Is life and peace (Rom. 8:6)**
Is hostile against God (Rom 8:7)	Meets the requirements of the Law (Rom 8:4)
Cannot please God (Rom 8:8)	**Gives life to your mortal body (Rom. 8:11)**

Can you find more comparisons?

As you go about today, be aware of your choices and which nature they fall under.

Daily Prayer: *Lord, I praise You for You alone know me and love me, faults and all. Help me, O God, to stop this cycle of sinful desire, help me to turn to You the moment it enters my mind. Turn my eyes and ears towards You so that I may hear Your voice every day. Amen.*

What thoughts came to mind as you worked on today's lesson? Be prepared to share:

Session 2: Day 4 – Temptation: Good Gifts
James 1:17
"Every good gift and every perfect gift is from above, and comes down from the Father of lights, with whom there is no variation or shadow of turning."

1. "Every good and perfect gift comes from above (God) . . . Father of lights. . . " (**DD** – Research "light" or "lights." What do you find?) What gifts has God given to you?

2. Have you ever given a gift to someone and couldn't wait until they opened it? Do you remember feeling the excitement growing inside with anticipation of their reaction? Share that moment with us.

Did you get the reaction you had hoped for? How did that make you feel?

3. Consider how God must have felt when He offered you the gift of His Son. . . and you accepted! Close your eyes and think of His face (please don't get legalistic on me, I know "no one" has seen the face of God, just imagine. . .) See Him smiling with anticipation of you removing the wrapper of salvation. . . stay in this moment. . . now, remember how you felt when you opened your heart to Him, and write those feelings here:

How have those feelings changed? Explain:

    During our family Christmas party one year, we each brought a gift, placed it under my brother's tree, and then drew numbers to see who would select their gift first. Everyone wanted the number *one* because it gave you the option of choosing again after everyone else had a shot, and yes, we would steal the gifts from each other until it was in the hands of the third owner. . . then it was frozen. Well this particular year I decided to be a bit conniving and I wrapped the gifts we brought in non-traditional ways, I didn't use pink for a girl or blue for a boy. This proved to be a source of frustration for my nephew Lane.

The manly man that he is, Lane chose a plain un-frilly package and wound up with a very feminine water pitcher, it screamed early Victorian era with ladies in hoopskirts abounding. Keeping a stiff upper lip, amid the outbursts of laughter coming from his male counterparts, he sat and silently prayed for someone to steal his *prize*. My son Sammie stood promptly when his number was called. After a few moments of bending and leaning to survey all his options (we had a strict no shaking allowed policy) he reached out and snatched up a lovely pink floral gift bag with matching tissue delicately peeking over the brim. Every mouth dropped wide open when he pulled out a three piece Winchester knife set. Laughter rang to the rafters when Lane, Sammie's older cousin by at least ten years, stood to his feet and yelled, "How is that possible? Girls don't use knives like that!"

When asked why he picked a girly looking bag Sammie replied, "I wasn't really looking at the color, I was going by the size of the bag. This one felt right."

Lane was surprised because the packaging didn't match the content. This happens to us in everyday life doesn't it? Sometimes we choose to only open gifts when they look like they *fit* us. In this case Lane learned, never judge a gift by its packaging.

4. Is "Every good and every perfect gift. . . " always something pleasant? Explain your answer.

5. James mentions there is no turning of shadow, no variation from the Father of lights, meaning everything we receive from God is good. Do we always see the good in life situations? Why or why not?

As you go about your day think of ways you can be a gift to others.

Daily Prayer: *Praise You Lord for Your gift is perfect. Thank You for choosing me to be the recipient of Your gift. Help me, O God, to cherish the memory of experiencing You for the very first time. Bring to my mind* *all You have gifted me with over the years. I pray my act of unwrapping your blessings is pleasing to you.* Amen.

What thoughts came to mind as you worked on today's lesson? Be prepared to share:

Session 2: Day 5 – Temptation: God's Will
James 1:18
"*Of His own will He brought us forth by the word of truth, that we might be a kind of first fruits of His creatures.*"

1. "*Of His own will. . .* " Who is this passage talking about? Explain.

2. "*. . . He brought us forth by the word of truth . . .* " What does this mean to you? (**DD** – Look up scripture explaining the "word of truth")

3. Explain what "first fruits" means to you. (**DD** – Find scripture that defines first fruits)

4. Do you give *first fruits* to God? Explain how you do.

5. How does your life reflect God's *first fruits*?

As you go about your day, ask God to expose *desires* that are not of Him. Recall and write down what you learn.

Daily Prayer: *Precious Father, thank you for this week. Thank you for opening my eyes to who You are and how much You love me. Help me, Lord, to hunger for You and Your Word. Help me to feel comfortable with the ladies in my small group. Give me the words I need to share and ears to hear as others share. Help me to be sensitive to Your Spirit daily... in Jesus name,* Amen.

What thoughts came to mind as you worked on today's lesson? Be prepared to share.

> # Session 3:
> # Reflection:
> # Showing Who
> # You Serve

"Did you ever wonder if the person in the puddle is real, and you're just a reflection of him?"
Bill Watterson

Session 3: Reflection: Showing Who You Serve

Weekly Reading: James 1:19-27 NKJV *"So then my beloved brethren, let every man be swift to hear, slow to speak, slow to wrath; for the wrath of man does not produce the righteousness of God. Therefore lay aside all filthiness and overflow of wickedness, and receive with meekness the implanted word, which is able to save your souls. But be doers of the word, and not hearers only, deceiving yourselves. For if anyone is a hearer of the word and not a doer, he is like a man observing his natural face in a mirror; for he observes himself, goes away, and immediately forgets what kind of man he was. But he who looks into the perfect law of liberty and continues in it, and is not a forgetful hearer but a doer of the work, this one will be blessed in what he does. If anyone among you thinks he is religious, and does not bridle his tongue but deceives his own heart, this one's religion is useless. Pure and undefiled religion before God and the Father is this: to visit orphans and widows in their trouble, and to keep oneself unspotted from the world."*

Take a minute and read through this passage of scripture, if you use a different translation, underline where the two have different words and phrases of significance. Do any of the differences stand out to you? Why?

Session 3: Day 1 – Reflection: Servant of the World
James 1:19-21

"So then my beloved brethren, let every man be swift to hear, slow to speak, slow to wrath; for the wrath of man does not produce the righteousness of God. Therefore lay aside all filthiness and overflow of wickedness, and receive with meekness the implanted word, which is able to save your souls."

1. Can you hear the heart of James in this verse? When he calls you *beloved* brethren, how does that make you feel?

2. List the names of fellow believers you would call *beloved*. Why did they make the list?

3. James gives us a three-part directive. How would you rank your obedience to the following? (0 – 5) 0 is least compliant; 5 is very compliant.

- Be. . . Swift to hear ____
- Be. . . Slow to speak ____
- Be. . . Slow to wrath ____

Does one of the three stand out as more of a challenge? Explain.

4. **Wrath**: *strong anger, often with a desire for revenge. in some beliefs, God's punishment for sin. the vengeance, punishment, or destruction wreaked by somebody in anger.* If applicable, which of these definitions most reflects your heart right now? How has *wrath* impacted this season of your life?

5. *". . . for the wrath of man does not produce the righteousness of God,"* what is righteousness? (**DD** look up scripture to support your answer)

6. How are we to *". . . lay aside all filthiness and overflow of wickedness?"* What does this mean?

7. When James uses the word *meekness* in this verse, what does it mean to you?

Do you struggle with meekness? Explain

8. We are instructed to receive with meekness the implanted word. Share how you view *implanted*.

9. Does *". . . receive with meekness the implanted word, which is able to save your souls"* have a double meaning here? Explain your answer

As you go about today, listen more, speak less, and chose meekness over wrath. Write down how this approach worked for you.

☺ Thank you for choosing to dig deeper into God's word. . . Linda

Daily Prayer: *Lord, help me today, in Your power, to be—swift to hear, slow to speak and slow to wrath. Open my ears to be sensitive to Your mighty words, close my mouth if my desire to speak is not pure, and cause me to breathe deep Your spirit when I am provoked to anger. Amen.*

Session 3: Day 2 – Reflection: Servant of the Word
James 1:22-24
"But be doers of the word, and not hearers only, deceiving yourselves. For if anyone is a hearer of the word and not a doer, he is like a man observing his natural face in a mirror; for he observes himself, goes away, and immediately forgets what kind of man he was."

1. What does " be doers of the word, and not hearers only. . . " mean to you?

2. **Deceive:** *to mislead or deliberately hide the truth from somebody; to convince yourself of something that is not true.* How do we deceive ourselves concerning God's word?

    Growing up I struggled with self-esteem issues all through high school and into adulthood. I wore braces to *correct* my imperfect teeth, slathered myself with cortisone ointments to *control* a severe skin disorder, and dieted, sometimes to extremes, to *model* good health. When I looked in the mirror I was never satisfied. . . hair, skin, teeth, body. . . if one area was good another needed work. I never *felt* acceptable. I imagine you may have some idea about not feeling perfect.

3. Here is an interactive step; I hope you choose to do it. Put down the guide and look at your face in a mirror for about 2 minutes. Then come back and read the rest. (Please Don't read ahead!)

4. Do you think women have a challenge seeing themselves for who they really are? Explain your answer.

5. Think of five features that stood out to you as you looked in the mirror. List them here:

☺ From Linda: We will discuss this activity in small group. . . I pray you followed instructions.

6. Do you have any favorite scripture verses? List them here to share with the group.

As you go about today, ask the Lord to reveal Himself to you in multiple ways — in your home, at work, through your family and friends. If you think about it, write what you observe here.

Daily Prayer: *Praise You O God for You alone are worthy to be praised. Praise You for You are faithful. Praise You for You are trustworthy. Praise You for even though I was yet a sinner, You lifted me from the miry depths of sin mud and all to one day reside in Your presence. Praise You Lord for being the Father of Lights in my life.* Amen.

Write one "new" thought about anything you're led to:

Here is your mid-week H.U.G. (His **U**nfailing **G**race) from Brenda. . .

    Sometimes, I just feel tired. I don't want to do anything. I don't want to go anywhere. I don't want to answer the phone. I don't want to talk to my husband, my friends, my cat. I don't even want to turn on the TV. Have you ever felt like me?

When I'm overwhelmed with all the cares of life, sometimes I just want to check-out. I'm not saying for a long time, but just for a day or even two. Life has a way of making lots of noise.

Why don't I sit at His feet sooner?

Dear Father, God is always so patient with me. He beckons me to Him often, and yet I keep going on with all the other noises of life — moving constantly, talking without any purpose, watching things of no importance. He keeps trying; whispering for me to sit still, open His Word, and let Him refresh me. Finally, I do. Peace surrounds me. Love envelopes me. Joy fills me.

Thank you for loving me even with all the choices I make before I make the choice to be in your presence. You teach me so much about love and patience and self-control. Help me, Lord, to grow in your fruit. Sweet Holy Spirit teach me more and more about Jesus, so I can know more about the Father. Let me be like Jesus. Let the worries of this world depart from me, and let me focus on the things that glorify and bring honor to You. I lift up the ladies in the study and ask that you give them time to sit at your feet. I ask for your presence in all they do. Touch their relationships with you and with others, and let Your heart become their hearts. I pray for your divine touch in their bodies as well as in the lives of their loved ones. You are Jehovah Rophe and nothing is impossible for You. Continue to give them favor at their jobs. For those seeking employment, I pray for open doors for them. Mostly, Lord, I pray that each one will seek to be still and to grow in wisdom, discernment and revelation of your will for their lives.
In Jesus' name, Amen.

Session 3: Day 3 – Reflection: Doer of the Word
James 1:25

"But he who looks into the perfect law of liberty and continues in it, and is not a forgetful hearer but a doer of the work, this one will be blessed in what he does."

1. What does it mean to *look* into the "perfect law of liberty?" (**DD** – Research these in scripture. What can you find?)

How do you ". . . continue in it"?

2. *Look* in it, *continue* in it, and *do not forget what you heard* in it… can you recall any situation in the past 30 – 60 days when the Holy Spirit brought to your mind a scripture verse that you applied in that moment, for yourself or sharing with another? List as many as you remember and what resulted.

3. What things cause us to be *forgetful hearers*?

4. Do you consider yourself a "doer of the work"? Explain your answer:

5. Do you believe *everyone* has a ministry? Explain:

6. If God has given you a specific ministry share what it is. If you are not sure, list ways God has worked in your life this past year:

As you go about today, be aware of opportunities you have to minister to others.

Daily Prayer: *Praise You Abba! Give me the desire to look into who You are. Cause my spirit to hunger for You, O Lord, so I will continue to seek You. Do not let me forget Your words; bring them to my mind that I may meditate on them daily. Help me, Father, to do the work You desire of me. Make clear my path and understanding that I may serve You with all my being from this day forth. Amen.*

☺ From Linda: As we go through this study, ask God to grow you beyond your current level of understanding about Him, His word, and yourself.

Session 3: Day 4 – Reflection: Useless in the World
James 1:26

"If anyone among you thinks he is religious, and does not bridle his tongue but deceives his own heart, this one's religion is useless."

1. When you hear the word "religious" what <u>automatically</u> comes to mind? How does the *world* view religion? Is there a difference? (**DD** – Research "religion" in scripture. List what you find.)

2. Do you know anyone who has an *unbridled* tongue? Are you one of those people? What does *unbridled* mean?

3. What does scripture say about the tongue? (Job 6:23-25 NKJV; Job 27:3-5 NIV; Psalm 12:2-4 NKJV; Psalm 16:8-10 NIV)

4. What does " . . . deceives his own heart. . . " mean to you? List ways we deceive ourselves and others:

5. What is meant by *useless* in " . . . *this one's religion is useless?*"

As you go about your day, listen to the world around you. How do the *tongues* of others impact your life?

Daily Prayer: *Precious Jesus, I lift Your name as THE Name above all names. Thank You Father for giving me Your Word in flesh and in the Bible. Help me to be worthy of Your sacrifice, I know there is nothing I could ever do to earn my position in heaven, yet I desire to be the firstfruits of Your love that others will know You because they know me. Amen.*

Thoughts you might like to share in your small group:

Session 3: Day 5 – Reflection: Useful in the World
James 1:27

"Pure and undefiled religion before God and the Father is this: to visit orphans and widows in their trouble, and to keep oneself unspotted from the world."

1. *"Pure and undefiled religion. . ."* What do these terms mean to you? Explain.

2. *". . . to visit orphans and widows in their trouble. . ."* What does this mean to you?

(**DD** – Look up scripture concerning "orphans and widows.")

3. What activities are you as an individual or as a family currently doing to be an example of this scripture verse in your community or in the world?

4. If you are not currently doing anything, what could you do?

5. *"... to keep oneself unspotted from the world."?* Explain what this means to you.

6. How would you explain this passage of scripture to children in their language?

7. How would you explain this passage to a non-believer?

As you go about your day, take note of any *"Pure and undefiled religion"* opportunities you have. Did you respond? If so, how?

Daily Prayer: *Praise You O God for Your love knows no boundaries. Help me to see Your children who are in need, give me wisdom that I may know what to do and courage to take the steps needed to accomplish Your will in Jesus name,* Amen.

Session 4:
Impartiality:
Seeing Through
God's Eyes

"We have a spiritual 'implant' of the life of Jesus Christ within our bodies. This is actually Jesus in the person of the Holy Spirit."
Anne Graham Lotz

Session 4: Impartiality: Seeing Through God's Eyes

Weekly Reading: James 2:1-13 *" My brethren, do not hold the faith of our Lord Jesus Christ, the Lord of glory, with partiality. For if there should come into your assembly a man with gold rings, in fine apparel, and there should also come in a poor man in filthy clothes, and you pay attention to the one wearing the fine clothes and say to him, 'You sit here in a good place,' and say to the poor man, 'You stand there,' or, 'Sit here at my footstool,' have you not shown partiality among yourselves, and become judges with evil thoughts? Listen, my beloved brethren: Has God not chosen the poor of this world to be rich in faith and heirs of the kingdom which He promised to those who love Him? But you have dishonored the poor man. Do not the rich oppress you and drag you into the courts? Do they not blaspheme that noble name by which you are called? If you really fulfill the royal law according to the Scripture, 'You shall love your neighbor as yourself,' you do well; but if you show partiality, you commit sin, and are convicted by the law as transgressors. For whoever shall keep the whole law, and yet stumble in one point, he is guilty of all. For He who said, 'Do not commit adultery,' also said, 'Do not murder'. Now if you do not commit adultery, but you do murder, you have become a transgressor of the law. So speak and so do as those who will be judged by the law of liberty. For judgment is without mercy to the one who has shown no mercy. Mercy triumphs over judgment."*

Take a minute and read through this passage of scripture, if you use a different translation, underline where the two have different words and phrases of significance. Do any of the differences stand out to you? Why?

Session 4: Day 1 – Impartiality: External View
James 2:1-4

"My brethren, do not hold the faith of our Lord Jesus Christ, the Lord of glory, with partiality. For if there should come into your assembly a man with gold rings, in fine apparel, and there should also come in a poor man in filthy clothes, and you pay attention to the one wearing the fine clothes and say to him, 'You sit here in a good place,' and say to the poor man, 'You stand there,' or, "Sit here at my footstool,' have you not shown partiality among yourselves, and become judges with evil thoughts?"

If someone was asked to describe you, would they use words like, judgmental, biased, cliquey, or prejudice? My initial reaction is, "Oh my, I hope not."

    A few years back, our church experienced a rude awakening to the judgmental possibilities inside our sacred walls of *sanctuary*. It was an ordinary Sunday morning filled with the expected sights and sounds of families pouring into pews ripe with the hustle and bustle of getting little ones to sit quietly as we prepared to worship the Lord in harmony. But what happened next caused many to pause in our ceremonious behavior, pondering the truth set before us.
    Pastor stood in the pulpit and asked how everyone was feeling, "Did you have a safe trip into church today? Anything out of the ordinary happen? Did you notice this man sitting at our church entrance?" Immediately everyone turned to the rear of the sanctuary. . . a disheveled, dirty, smelly person was slowly making his way to the front of the church following the lead of our pastor. "Come down here my friend, I want to introduce you to our church family."
    Several members let out sighs of painful remorse, as the "man" removed his head covering to reveal himself as one of our deacons. Very early that morning, he had positioned himself at a prominent entrance to our church. Slumped on the steps where you would run into him if you weren't paying attention, he stayed waiting for someone, anyone to invite him in. My understanding is we did have one or two men approach him, but he remained as a test to see how many others would respond. Sadly, the masses passed him by, carefully stepping around as they went about their Sunday morning regimen. I didn't enter our church from that side, but I immediately wondered, "What would I have done?"

1. Do you feel your church could improve in making outsiders feel welcome? What are some things any church could do that would make YOU feel like planting your roots?

2. We really don't want to see ourselves as *judgmental* but if we are honest… come on now. Do you ever find yourself judging others because of their outside appearance? Explain

3. Another word that translates into impartiality is **neutrality**. We are asked to be neutral and non-judgmental in the church but to hold to strict standards in the world? Is this easy for you? (This one will be on the test. . . Linda ☺)

> **Impartiality**: not biased - *having no direct involvement or interest and not favoring one person or side more than another.*

4. Write down what you think about the author's comment, "... have you not shown partiality among yourselves, and become judges with evil thoughts?" (**DD** Look up scripture to support your answer.)

As you go about today, be alert to your response and the response of others to the *differences* in people. Write in the margin what you observe?

Daily Prayer: *Open the eyes of my heart Lord, I want to see others the way You see me.* Amen

☺ Give yourself a hug from me please. . . Linda

Session 4: Day 2 – Impartiality: Internal View
James 2:5-7

"Listen, my beloved brethren: Has God not chosen the poor of this world to be rich in faith and heirs of the kingdom which He promised to those who love Him? But you have dishonored the poor man. Do not the rich oppress you and drag you into the courts? Do they not blaspheme that noble name by which you are called?"

1. Do you hear the pleading in James voice? God really wants us to get this. It's kind of like when we look at our children or a family member in the eyes saying, "Are you listening?" Have you felt God pleading with you about a specific area of your life? Explain.

2. *"Has God not chosen the poor of this world to be rich in faith and heirs of the kingdom which He promised to those who love Him?"* How do you apply this scripture to your life? Fill in the following:

    What is the scripture saying? (Truth)

    What does it mean to me? (Your opinion)

    How does it apply to my season? (Relevance to your life now)

    Verses for review (Matthew 5:3; Is. 61:1; Luke 4:16-21; 7:22)

3. After last week's study, has your understanding of *loving God* changed? How?

4. How are the *poor* (Those who bow down to God) dishonored today?

5. Do you believe the *rich* (Those independent of God) are really as negative as scripture says here? Why or why not?

6. James mentions the *noble* name by which you are called. What names do you give to God? List them here.

As you go about today, ask the Father to show His heart to others through you.

Daily Prayer: *Praise You Lord that Your love can flow through me when I chose to love You. Help me to love You more so others can feel the warmth of Your embrace in all I do.* Amen.

Here is your mid-week H.U.G. (His **U**nfailing **G**race**) from Brenda…**

Hi Beautiful Woman of God,
    I pray your week is full of love for God and for others. Sometimes, I ponder the condition of Christians sharing the Gospel, and it makes me sad. What I see most of the time is a hesitancy to share Jesus with others. Many believe they don't have to tell people about Jesus, but rather their lives need to tell the message. That sounds good, but it's not what the Scripture says.

We can look at the disciples and see the instruction the Lord had for them.

In Mark 3:14, Jesus "appointed twelve —designating them apostles —that they might be with him and that he might send them out to preach..." Jesus also in Matthew 28:19 says, "Therefore go and make disciples of all nations, baptizing them in the name of the Father and of the Son and of the Holy Spirit, and teaching them to obey everything I have commanded you."

We are His modern-day disciples, and the task has not changed. In fact telling others about Jesus was the last thing He told his disciples before "He was taken up into heaven and sat at the right hand of God." The words He spoke were these, "Go into all the world and preach the good news to all creation." See the full account in Mark 16:14-19. Then in obedience to his teachings, in Act 5:42, we see the apostles, "Day after day, in the temple courts and from house to house, they never stopped teaching and proclaiming the good news that Jesus is the Christ."

The Lord knows that many people do good works, but good works alone do not mean a changed heart nor belief in God the Father, God the Son, and God the Holy Spirit. People with no belief in God can do good works or live a life that looks good to others. Thus, Christians who refuse to share Christ verbally may look just like a non-believer who lives a "good" life. What will make the unbeliever know he or she is a sinner and in need of a Savior? Without the message being heard, faith can not develop. Romans 10:17 says, "Consequently, faith comes from hearing the message, and the message is heard through the word of Christ." Paul goes on to say in Romans 10:14-15, "How, then, can they call on the one they have not believed in? And how can they believe in the one of whom they have not heard? And how can they hear without someone preaching to them? And how can they preach unless they are sent? As it is written, 'How beautiful are the feet of those who bring good news!'"

As with all things, there are usually two sides to the issue. Yes, actions do speak louder than words many times, but in terms of sharing Christ, we must first share Him verbally, and then follow-up with good deeds and living a good life. Genuine faith in Christ should always result in actions that are obedient to the teachings of Christ. James 1:22 says it best when he said, "Do not merely listen to the word...Do what it says." He then adds in 2 Timothy 4:1-2, "In the presence of God and of Christ Jesus, who will judge the living and the dead, and in view of his appearing and his kingdom, I give you this charge: Preach the Word; be prepared in season and out of season; correct, rebuke, and encourage — with great patience and careful instruction."

I pray we will see the urgency of preaching the Gospel. Christians can't afford to be hesitant. Today, may be someone's last day. In fact, the whole world's end may be today. What will be our response when we stand before Him and He asks us about our witness?

Dear Father,
I come before You with a heart of thanksgiving for all You have given us. Let us always be reminded of the gifts we have in You. Thank you, Lord, for Your presence and for guiding us to do Your will. Let our mouths always be ready to share the love of Jesus with others who are dying. Let us glorify You in our every action and in our speech. Teach us Your word and burn it on our hearts and minds, so we can recall it in our times of need. I lift up our ladies in the study and ask for Your hand to be upon them as well as on the lives of their friends, co-workers and families. We know you are capable of handling every situation and giving solutions for each need. Thank You for Your healing touch on physical as well as emotional and spiritual matters. You want us to be whole in You and to live out Holy lives in our thoughts and actions. Thank you that Your Holy Spirit teaches us. Protect us as we go about our lives doing the work You have called us to do. Let us be bold for You.

In His Name, the name above all names, Jesus Christ, Amen.

Session 4: Day 3 – Impartiality: Royal Law
James 2:8-10

"If you really fulfill the royal law according to the Scripture, 'You shall love your neighbor as yourself,' you do well; but if you show partiality, you commit sin, and are convicted by the law as transgressors. For whoever shall keep the whole law, and yet stumble in one point, he is guilty of all."

1. Why do we have such a hard time complying with the *"royal law?"*

   (Lev. 19:18; Matt. 5:43-45 – info on Royal law)

2. When do you find yourself more apt to show *partiality*? Why?

3. Many would not consider *"For whoever shall keep the whole law, and yet stumble in one point, he is guilty of all"* unfair. What do you think and why?

4. How would you encourage a sister who was struggling with this issue of "loving your neighbor. . . ?" See Gal. 5:13-15

☺ **Go Back and Check the Wisdom Chart**

As you go about today, write down Acts of Love you witness from others—be ready to share in group time.

Daily Prayer: *I praise You O God, that You love me regardless of how I treat You or Your children. But I know You are grieved when I turn from Your ways. Help me, Holy Spirit to love others through Your power, not my own.* Amen.

**Session 4: Day 4 – Impartiality: God's Commandments
James 2:11**
"For He who said, 'Do not commit adultery,' also said, 'Do not murder'. Now if you do not commit adultery, but you do murder, you have become a transgressor of the law. . ."

1. Do you consider all sin equal? Be ready to explain your answer.

2. How could we explain all sin as equal to non-believers? (**DD** – Find support scripture to accomplish this.)

3. Which of the Ten Commandment (Exodus 20:1-17) is the most challenging for you? Why?

> Write a New Thought you've received this week:

As you go about your day ask the Holy Spirit to reveal His *truth* about why you struggle with the Commandment(s) you do. Write what He gives you here:

Daily Prayer: *Abba, give me time on Your lap today. Help me as I choose to dig deeper into my relationship with You. As the world seeks to draw me away, pierce my heart with a renewed hunger for You. I do so very much desire to know You more. In the precious name of My Lord, Jesus Christ,* Amen.

☺ Thank you for praying for me. . . Linda

Session 4: Day 5 – Impartiality: Law of Liberty
James 2:12-13
"So speak and so do as those who will be judged by the law of liberty. For judgment is without mercy to the one who has shown no mercy. Mercy triumphs over judgment."

1. What does God want us to hear in this passage, "*So speak and do so as those who will be judged by the law of liberty*"? Is He telling us to be cautious, bold, quiet, or what?

2. Have you heard of the law of liberty before? What do you think this means?

3. "*. . . judgment is without mercy to one who has shown no mercy . . .*" What does this mean to you?

(**DD** – Give us some background on *mercy*)

4. Has mercy triumphed over judgment in your life? Explain.

As you go about your day, ask the Holy Spirit to show you where He has been merciful in your life. Share if you are led to do so:

Daily Prayer: *Grant me deeper insight into You Father God, through the power of the Holy Spirit within me. Open my spiritual eyes. . . reveal to me, Your holiness, that I may release all I am to Your service. Amen.*

Session 5: Faith: Walking The Walk

"Without faith a man can do nothing; with it all things are possible."
Sir William Osler

Session 5: Faith: Walking The Walk

Weekly Reading: James 2:14-26 NKJV *"What does it profit, my brethren, if someone says he has faith but does not have works? Can faith save him? If a brother or sister is naked and destitute of daily food, and one of you says to them, 'Depart in peace, be warmed and filled,' but you do not give them the things which are needed for the body, what does it profit? Thus also faith by itself, if it does not have works, is dead. But someone will say, 'You have faith, and I have works.' Show me your faith without your works, and I will show you my faith by my works. You believe that there is one God. You do well. Even the demons believe— and tremble! But do you want to know, O foolish man, that faith without works is dead? Was not Abraham our father justified by works when he offered Isaac his son on the altar? Do you see that faith was working together with his works, and by works faith was made perfect? And the Scripture was fulfilled which says, 'Abraham believed God, and it was accounted to him for righteousness.' And he was called the friend of God. You see then that a man is justified by works, and not by faith only. Likewise, was not Rahab the harlot also justified by works when she received the messengers and sent them out another way? For as the body without the spirit is dead, so faith without works is dead also."*

Take a minute and read through this passage of scripture, if you use a different translation, underline where the two have different words and phrases of significance. Do any of the differences stand out to you? Why?

Session 5: Day 1 – Faith: Tell or Show?
James 2:14
"What does it profit, my brethren, if someone says he has faith but does not have works? Can faith save him?"

1. "What does it profit. . . " can be reworded to, what good is it. How would you answer the question, "What good is it to say you have faith when you don't act like it?"

2. Have you ever known someone who turned you off from *religion* because they were hypocritical in their faith-walk? Share your experience with the group:

3. Write down your feelings about the following text: "Can faith save him?"

As you go about your day, be aware of your actions. What are you doing to reflect Christ in you?

☺ Give yourself a hug from me please. . . Linda

Daily Prayer: *Father, create in me a deep desire to be Your hands and feet this week. Show me the path You have set before me. . .* Amen

Session 5: Day 2 – Faith: Passive or Active?
James 2:15-17

"If a brother or sister is naked and destitute of daily food, and one of you says to them, 'Depart in peace, be warmed and filled,' but you do not give them the things which are needed for the body, what does it profit? Thus also faith by itself, if it does not have works, is dead."

> **Naked:** unarmed and defenseless; lacking the usual covering or protection; not covered by clothing, especially having no clothing on any part of the body
>
> **Destitute:** lacking all money, resources, and possessions necessary for subsistence

1. Notice that *naked* doesn't always mean without clothes. What does it feel like to be *naked* in today's society? Explain:

2. Have you ever been in a situation where you were destitute? Did God place someone in your path to minister to you? Explain.

3. Do you or your family have a *mission of service*? If yes, what is it? If no, what would you like it to be?

4. Is it the church's responsibility to take care of the poor and the widows or ours as individuals? Explain your answer.

(**DD** - Find scripture on this subject.) ☺ From Linda: We will discuss this question in small group. . .

5. Again James shares, " . . . faith by itself, if it does not have works, is dead." Why is God making this such a big point?

As you go about today, ask yourself or talk to your family about getting involved with a mission-of-service. Write what you decide here.

Daily Prayer: *Praise You, Lord because You saw me in my nakedness and You clothed me with Your righteousness. Help me, O God, to reach out to others, not in word but in deed to reflect Your grace in my life. Amen.*

Here is your mid-week H.U.G. (His **U**nfailing **G**race**) from Brenda. . .**

Be blessed in Jesus! He is our hope! Did you know that God says, "Fear not," 365 times in the Bible? He repeats himself because we need to hear it. The LORD doesn't want us to live in fear. He knows we get afraid, anxious and worried, but His hope for us is that we will trust Him. His desire is for us to let Him be so big in our lives that we know He is greater than our greatest fears.

As most of us know, fear doesn't fight fair. It simply turns our small worries into something big and frightening and heart-wrenching. A small concern can become a mountain because we have allowed the evil one to trick our minds and to focus on the concern versus Jesus. Once we get our eyes off of Him, fear grows big, bigger, and biggest until it's so consuming, we believe the worst is going to happen to us.

What we have to do is keep our focus on trusting God and the many promises He has made us. He never leaves us nor forsakes us. We are His children. We can call on Him. He is our deliverer. He is our strength. He does not lie. He loves us. He is the Good Shepherd. He knows exactly where we are at all times, and He can find us. Be encouraged to get into the Word and read His many promises of encouragement to you, His beloved. Trust in His promises like Isaiah 41:13 where He says, "For I am the LORD, your God, who takes hold of your right hand and says to you, Do not fear; I will help you."

Break the cycle of letting fear reign in your life. Quit relying on your own means or strength as your means and strength are not sufficient. Only Christ is sufficient. He is enough. You can trust Him. He won't let you down. Begin today!

Dear Father,
We come humbly to Your throne room and give praise to You. You are the Beginning and the End, the Alpha and the Omega. You are all-knowing, all-present, and all-powerful. Nothing and no one has more authority than You do. Thank You, Lord, for Your unending love for us. I lift up the needs of every woman in this study. You are so good to Your children. A simple prayer like, "Help me," can warrant a thousand angels to attend to those who are yours. I ask that You help them today, this very hour, to know the depth of Your love and the many things You have planned for those who trust in You. I ask You to heal the sufferings of Your people, to heal them from the inside-out, to quench the feelings of despair and loss, to strengthen their love towards spouses and co-workers, to remind them that they are set apart for a purpose. I ask that they be not fearful of what man can do, or of their finances, or of their travels, but I ask that they boldly ask of You to show Yourself in all things. Let them "lean not on their own understanding," but to "trust in the Lord with all their hearts." You will be faithful and prove Yourself strong in every situation. Let us be reminded that Your timing and Your means of delivery are perfect. Encourage us, Father, with Your strong right hand and lift us from the things that are entangling us with fear, doubt, anger, and impure thoughts and actions. We need You, Lord. We worship You, Lord. We give our needs over to You and accept Your perfect answer for them all. In Jesus' name, Amen.

Session 5: Day 3 – Faith: Knowledge or Belief?
James 2:18-19

"But someone will say, 'You have faith, and I have works.' Show me your faith without your works, and I will show you my faith by my works. You believe that there is one God. You do well. Even the demons believe—and tremble!"

> **Work(s)** – the duties or activities that are part of a job or occupation; something that has been done or made as part of a job or as a result of effort or activity requiring skill.

1. Have you ever experienced a situation when a non-Christian ministered to you in a time of need? Explain how that made you feel.

2. Read Luke 10:25-37 and see a story of an un-churched person who helped a person in need. What does that story mean to you in this season of your life?

(**DD** find information on cults who use this approach to win converts)

3. Do you believe Christians are judged <u>unfairly</u> by their actions or lack of action? Why?

4. Do you think we are to look at *works* as though it were part of our *job* as a Christian? Explain.

☺ You are doing great! Thank you for being a part of this study.

5. Where do our *skills* come from to do good works for God?

6. *"You believe that there is one God. You do well. Even the demons believe—and tremble!"* What is the truth you hear in this verse? How does it apply to you right now?

7. Demons have belief or knowledge, but *we* are to have faith. Why is faith more powerful?

As you go about today, think on the ways God has given you opportunity to act on your belief. Praise Him for opening those doors.

Daily Prayer: *Lord, help me to be more than knowledgeable of Your Word. Deepen my understanding by showing me the power of belief this week. Praise You God for Your love and for the women of this group. Keep everyone safe and help each of us to see You clearly at work in our lives.* Amen.

Session 5: Day 4 – Faith: Mature or Immature Faith?
James 2:20-23
"But do you want to know, O foolish man, that faith without works is dead? Was not Abraham our father justified by works when he offered Isaac his son on the altar? Do you see that faith was working together with his works, and by works faith was made perfect? And the Scripture was fulfilled which says, 'Abraham believed God, and it was accounted to him for righteousness.' And he was called the friend of God."

1. Does God call all of us out to *sacrifice* something precious in our lives for Him? Be ready to explain your answer.

2. Who is James speaking to here, ". . . O foolish man. . . "? (**DD** – Find scripture references to *fool* or *foolish*.)

3. Does this passage in Eph. 2:9-10 conflict with Paul, who insisted that a person was justified by faith alone? Explain?

4. James tells us *"Scripture was fulfilled. . . "* speaking of Genesis 15:6. Why is it important for you to know this?

5. Do you consider yourself a *friend* of God? Explain

As you go about today, get skinny with the Spirit and ask Him to show you areas of your life you need to place on the altar before Him.

Daily Prayer: *Dear God, precious Savior, wonderful Counselor, I sometimes sing that I have a friend in Jesus or that I am a friend of God. Help me to really believe what I profess with my mouth. Turn me away from those times when I just say the words, create in me a heart pleasing to You. A heart that sings a fresh song to You daily. In Jesus name, Amen.*

☺ I am praying for you today. Thank you for praying for me. . . Linda

Session 5: Day 5 – Faith: Talk or Walk?
James 2:24-26

"You see then that a man is justified by works, and not by faith only. Likewise, was not Rahab the harlot also justified by works when she received the messengers and sent them out another way? For as the body without the spirit is dead, so faith without works is dead also."

1. Do you agree with the biblical application of *justified*? Write out your reasoning for *works*.

> **Justified**: - having an acceptable reason for the action taken; acceptable or reasonable in the circumstances.
>
> **Biblical application**: Made just in God's eyes, acceptable by Him. God is Just... His justice is satisfied in Jesus Christ.

2. Compare Rahab's words in Joshua 2:9-11 to Joshua 1:2, 11, 13. What traits are shown about Rahab?

What spiritual insight does Rahab also reveal? See Joshua 2:11 for additional insight.

Rahab's actions were punishable by death, yet she not only recognized God for who He is, (when she called Him Yahweh it was a confession of her faith) she put feet to her faith with actions.

3. Are you feeling led to hang out the scarlet-cord-of-faith? Is there something you know God desires of you that might have devastating results? Explain.

4. *". . . the body without the spirit is dead, so faith without works is dead also."* What does this mean to you?

5. How would you use this verse to encourage a woman who has a less than perfect past? Explain

Go back through this week's study and **find two things you want to discuss during group time.** This can include your response to a question, your research findings, or maybe a question that you want to discuss with the group. Mark them with a star.

As you go about your day, prayerfully consider your day-to-day actions. Are you walkin' out or just talkin' about your faith-walk?

Daily Prayer: *The heavens declare Your name O God, in all I see, hear, smell, taste or touch I witness the magnitude of Your works. Increase my faith that I may be of greater use to You, fill me to overflowing with a hunger for Your word and a desire to be Your hands and feet in this season of my life. Believing You to give wisdom when it is asked in accordance to Your will, I ask of You now, in Jesus name,* Amen.

Session 6: Words: Taming the Tongue

"Sweet words are like honey, a little may refresh, but too much gluts the stomach."
Anne Bradstreet

Session 6: Words: Taming the Tongue

Weekly Reading: James 3:1-12 *"My brethren, let not many of you become teachers, knowing that we shall receive a stricter judgment. For we all stumble in many things. If anyone does not stumble in word, he is a perfect man, able also to bridle the whole body. Indeed, we put bits in horses' mouths that they may obey us, and we turn their whole body. Look also at ships: although they are so large and are driven by fierce winds, they are turned by a very small rudder wherever the pilot desires. Even so the tongue is a little member and boasts great things. See how great a forest a little fire kindles! And the tongue is a fire, a world of iniquity. The tongue is so set among our members that it defiles the whole body, and sets on fire the course of nature; and it is set on fire by hell. For every kind of beast and bird, of reptile and creature of the sea, is tamed and has been tamed by mankind. But no man can tame the tongue. It is an unruly evil, full of deadly poison. With it we bless our God and Father, and with it we curse men, who have been made in the similitude of God. Out of the same mouth proceed blessing and cursing. My brethren, these things ought not to be so. Does a spring send forth fresh water and bitter from the same opening? Can a fig tree, my brethren, bear olives, or a grapevine bear figs? Thus no spring yields both salt water and fresh."*

Take a minute and read through this passage of scripture. If you use a different translation, underline where the two have different words and phrases of significance. Do any of the differences stand out to you? Why?

☺ **Reminder**, underline or highlight words and write in the margins of your Bible anything that stands out, include the date for future reference. . . HUGS (**H**is **U**nfailing **G**race is **S**ufficient)

Session 6: Day 1 – Words: Listening 101
James 3:1-2

"My brethren, let not many of you become teachers, knowing that we shall receive a stricter judgment. For we all stumble in many things. If anyone does not stumble in word, he is a perfect man, able also to bridle the whole body."

1. What does this scripture mean to you? If a teacher is held to a stricter judgment, then how does it make you feel about sharing God's word? What is the difference in witnessing and teaching in your view? (**DD -** Find scripture on this subject. . . teachers, witnessing, etc.)

2. How does *"For we all stumble in many things"* speak to you? Have you experienced a *stumble* in life? Please share with the group if you feel led.

3. *"If anyone does not stumble in word, he is a perfect man, also able to bridle the whole body."* Do you recognize the concept being projected here? If it were possible for a man to control what he says 100% of the time, we will see proof in his walk. Is it possible to be perfect? Explain.

4. Are there people or people-groups we try to place in a pedestal-worthy category? Explain.

When I think of the world's view of *pedestal-worthy* people, I immediately see pastors, leaders of countries, celebrities, and such. As a Christian, I know better (insert tongue in cheek) —no one is worthy of a higher position than our Heavenly Father. But, if I may be truthful and extremely transparent, there are certain people I have held to a higher standard for years, to our relational detriment.

Unintentionally I had built a huge pedestal and placed my husband, children, siblings and parents up on the higher levels. In reality I was setting them up for a great fall, and when the falls came, instead of being the loving nurturing wife, mother, sister, or daughter, I found myself pointing a finger of judgment and harboring feelings of hurt, anger, and resentment. Mind you, if I was sought out by a friend to offer *wisdom* concerning the misbehavior or attitude of their loved one, my *first* response would have been one of mercy. Oh I can hear me now, "Come on Suzy, do you really think Bob would go out of his way to make you feel rejected? I'm sure he is overwhelmed by his work and isn't thinking clearly. Why don't you sit down tonight and ask Bob about his job so he can talk it out… and remember Suzy no pointing fingers or saying, 'If you loved me, you should know better.' Just speak with a calm voice and share feelings, then let the Holy Spirit work."

I stand amazed and saddened that I offer more grace to strangers than I do my family and loved ones. . . What about you?

5. What happens to people who are placed on pedestals? How can we keep from placing others or ourselves up there? Give some practical examples.

As you go about your day, consider your words. Do they edify others?

☺ Umm, yeah! Give yourself a hug, squeeze tightly. . . Linda

Daily Prayer: *Lord, I seek Your anointing to go deeper as I study from Your word this week. Help me to speak words that would bring glory to You. Close my mouth if my words are not pleasing to You. Amen.*

Session 6: Day 2 – Words: Taking Charge
James 3:3-5a
"Indeed, we put bits in horses' mouths that they may obey us, and we turn their whole body. Look also at ships: although they are so large and are driven by fierce winds, they are turned by a very small rudder wherever the pilot desires. Even so the tongue is a little member and boasts great things."

Have you ever seen a horse's "bit"? It is a small, narrow, yet heavy, flat piece of metal with a loop on each end. Once placed at the back of the horse's mouth, in a space that seems to be created perfectly for it, the *bit* has the ability to control the horse. Leather reins are attached to the loops and the rider holds the reins to guide the horse. Amazing how something small in the mouth of such a large animal can have so much power. It's as though God knew how useful this creature could be once controlled, such immense power put to good use for mankind.

My experience with horses is they all have a mind of their own. From one breed to another, their temperament can be willing to comply or rebellious to the end. Our *Tennessee Walker*, Big John, stood 14 hands high weighed around 1200 pounds, but was a gentle giant. John had the ability to do whatever he wanted to, yet, his temperament was ever compliant to his master's will. Even if he was caught in barbed-wire, he would stand calmly waiting for Sam or me to come and free him -- he was quite the odd duck... er horse.

Animals do not have the ability to make a conscience decision, but rather they behave based on instinct. Man on the other hand, has a choice... to speak, listen, and obey or not.

1. Yesterday's reading said a "perfect man" could bridle his entire body. If we agree there is no perfect man, how is it feasible to believe we can comply with God's high expectations?

2. Consider this verse, "*[5] Even so the tongue is a little member and boasts great things."* **Boasts**: an act of talking with excessive pride and self-satisfaction. When are we most susceptible to boastful talk?

3. Is there an area in your life where *pride* has a negative hold? If you are willing, share this with the group. Be ready to discuss why you feel this way and be open to the thoughts of the group as to how pride can be overcome.

4. *Self-satisfaction* is a condoned emotion in today's society. Share examples in your small-group time. Why do you believe Satan uses this emotion as much as he does?

As you go about today, make note of prideful or self-satisfying actions you take. Make a mental note of the surroundings or situation. Share what you observed. Was it different from any other day?

Daily Prayer: *Open my eyes and ears O Lord that I may be aware of my words and actions. Help me in every moment to not be prideful of myself. Draw my eyes upward to Your grace that I may seek to bring You glory in all I do.* Amen.

Here is your mid-week H.U.G. (His **U**nfailing **G**race**) from Brenda. . .**

Dear Friend and Fellow Believer in the Lord Jesus Christ,

    I pray you have a week full of splendor and God's miracles.
    Are you living an abundant life or a defeated life? As Christians, we should be living an abundant life, but sadly many are not. Jesus certainly wants us to enjoy our lives every day. John 10:10b says, "I came that they may have and enjoy life, and have it in abundance." That means "to the full, till it overflows."
    I've met a lot of angry, bitter, frustrated and hurt people who confess Jesus as Lord. And yet, they live in a state of perpetual defeat. Jesus suffered, died, and then rose again, so those who put their faith in Him, can experience victory, freedom and abundance as well. But, the key is applying Jesus' truth to one's life.
    It makes me sad to see so many brothers and sisters in the Lord being robbed of their promised lot on earth. The reason is simple--they

have given the devil too much influence and power in their lives. We need to be on constant guard. The first part of John 10:10 tells the flip side to God's plan of abundance for His children. Remember, "the thief comes only to steal and kill and destroy" (John 10:10a).

A Christian who is living a defeated life has let Satan outwit him or her and gain a position of advantage. 2 Cor 2:11 says, "in order that satan might not outwit us. For we are not unaware of his schemes."

If you're feeling as though you're living a defeated life, you can change the course of your day. Ignore satan's schemes and plans. Remove satan's game card from your mind. Recall the Scriptures and know the Truth--satan has already been defeated. As a believer, you have the Greater One living inside you.

The next time satan knocks at your mind, let him know his end is near. Don't give him any encouragement by giving him an audience. Instead, go to the cross. Jesus runs satan off every time.

Dear Father,

We come to You with grateful hearts, always glad to be in Your presence. Thank you for giving us the mind of Christ. Thank you for the gift of Your Holy Spirit who guides and directs our steps to be more like Jesus.

Teach us to obey Your voice. Let us not be slow in doing what You call us to do. Protect us from thoughts and actions that are not pleasing to You. Let us discern all situations and respond in ways that show Your wisdom. We strive to be Your witnesses in all matters.

Lord, we ask that You incline Your ear to the ladies in this study. We ask for Your continued grace on their lives and on the lives of their loved ones. Heal afflictions, broken marriages and hurt emotions. Give them strength to endure and increase the fruit of patience and self-control. Provide finances for Your children by opening doors that seem closed and showing new avenues to pursue. Lord, You own all things, and we know You supply all we need. We ask for favor for those who need employment to find jobs that are edifying to You and perfect for their gifts and talents. We know nothing is impossible for You, and we trust Your realm of influence on the employers. If you want others to step out and begin a dream You have placed on his/her heart, we pray for boldness to do the calling You have given. Thank you, Father, that you are faithful to fulfill all areas of our lives. We love You. We honor You. We give You praise. We look with anticipated hearts to see how You will work in this prayer. In Jesus' Name, Amen.

Session 6: Day 3 –Words: Damage Control
James 3:5b-6
"See how great a forest a little fire kindles! And the tongue is a fire, a world of iniquity. The tongue is so set among our members that it defiles the whole body, and sets on fire the course of nature; and it is set on fire by hell."

    I spent a lot of my childhood in the great outdoors: living on a farm, participating in the Girl Scouts, hiking, camping and fishing. Learning the proper way to start a fire for the optimum-burn is a lesson I'll never forget. You must use just the right amount of kindling to get the fire going. Kindling can vary depending on what's available, but for the most part, we used dry loose-woven scraps of wood or brush. Sometimes we used newspaper tied in knots. It's the proper airflow through the kindling that created the slow burn that would ignite the larger pieces of wood, thus building a fire that would last the night.

    The visual that comes to mind when I read this passage is the devastation I have witnessed along the countryside from uncontrolled forest fires. I remember when "Smokey the Bear" would show up on TV or in school, reminding me, "Only YOU can prevent forest fires." Along with the words, I remember seeing animals running from the flames and even pictures of those who did not make it out of the forest. My heart ached for those poor creatures, causing me to be even more determined to do my part concerning proper disposal of campfires, matches, and my parent's cigarettes.

    As passionate as I was about saving the animals, I never considered my *words* having the same impact as that of an uncontrolled fire, burning up everyone in its path. I have numerous memories that expose the charring effects of my words on others, especially the ones I claim to love. Can you remember times when your words have had a destructive outcome?

1. List the names of those whom your words have caused pain.

Ask the Lord to forgive you for those you have hurt. Consider taking action by calling or sending a note to them asking for forgiveness. Allow the Spirit to direct your path, not everyone will be led to make personal contact.

2. Can you think of people whose words have caused *you* pain? List their names here.

Ask God to give you the desire to forgive them. On a separate piece of paper, write a letter of forgiveness to these people. You don't need to mail it as writing it down alone may give you release from the evil ones grip. (**DD** - Find scriptures on forgiveness)

3. The scripture study also says, "*And the tongue is a fire, a world of iniquity.*" Why do you think the tongue has such power? List some personal examples to show the power of your own tongue in a positive way and also in a negative way.

4. **Iniquity:** – immoral or grossly unfair behavior. Where do we see the iniquity of the tongue in our everyday life? (Schools, in the home, churches, etc.) Explain the "fire" effect in these areas.

☺ **I am so glad you are going through this study with me! Thank you.**

5. Explain what this verse means to you, "*The tongue is so set among our members that it defiles the whole body, and sets on fire the course of nature; and it is set on fire by hell.*"

As you go about today, be swift to listen to the Holy Spirit and allow Him to have full rein on your tongue.

Daily Prayer: *Lord, You alone are worthy of praise. You alone seek to know me beyond the surface of my existence. Praise You, for You are holy. You are forgiving. You are pure of spirit. Guide my thoughts, Father, moment-by-moment that I may walk faith-full during this season of my life. Help me to stay on the path of Your will. Place in me the spiritual "bit" of willingness that I may give myself over to you fully. In the name of my savior Jesus Christ,* Amen.

Session 6: Day 4 – Words: Taming the Tongue
James 3:7-9

"For every kind of beast and bird, of reptile and creature of the sea, is tamed and has been tamed by mankind. But no man can tame the tongue. It is an unruly evil, full of deadly poison. With it we bless our God and Father, and with it we curse men, who have been made in the similitude of God."

1. How do we know this to be true, *"⁷ For every kind of beast and bird, of reptile and creature of the sea, is tamed and has been tamed by mankind"*? Why is it relevant to you today? *See Genesis 1:26-28

2. Do you find, as I do, the effective visual impact of James' word choice concerning the tongue, *"It is an unruly evil, full of deadly poison"?* Look up Genesis 3:1-5, paying particular attention to the word-choices of Satan. Why did he have such control over Eve? List some of his words that deceived her and why they did (**DD** – Find scripture references to "the tongue" or "our words.")

3. Are your mental words any less poisonous even if you do not curse or belittle people out loud? Explain.

4. How can we lead by example the proper use of our words with our children or in the presence of non-believers?

5. Do you have any stories of when your words gave way to repressed feelings, exposing distasteful truths? How did it impact those around you?

6. If *"...no man can tame the tongue..."* how can we overcome the desire to speak evil? Look back in our study for the answer. Share scriptures to back up your thoughts.

As you go about today, speak less and listen. Listen and listen more.

Daily Prayer: *Abba, thank you for making room for me on Your lap today. Provide for me the opportunity to see You at work through my words. Reveal when I am crossing the line of unworthy talk and help me to refrain that I may be a reflection of You. In Jesus name,* Amen.

☺ I pray for God to reveal His glory to you today... Linda

Session 6: Day 5 – Words: Producing Fruit
James 3:10-12
"*Out of the same mouth proceed blessing and cursing. My brethren, these things ought not to be so. Does a spring send forth fresh water and bitter from the same opening? Can a fig tree, my brethren, bear olives, or a grapevine bear figs? Thus no spring yields both salt water and fresh.*"

1. What does our speech reveal about us? (See Matthew 12:36-37 for Truth.) What does this Matthew passage mean to you personally?

"*My brethren, these things ought not to be so.*" My first thought is, "Tell me it isn't so!" But in reality, I know that it is. My mouth can praise God in one moment and scream ill-will to someone else in the next. One of the best examples of expressing ill-will towards others often occurs when driving in the car.

Have you ever been in a hurry to get somewhere when not one, but two or three of the slowest-cars-in-the-world makes their way in front of you? No matter what you do to persuade them to get over they remain steadfast in the fast lane. How do you respond? Some of the most teachable moments for our children, as far as learning "new words" occurred while their dad was driving. Enough said!

I must say as my faith-walk has matured, I am more willing to give way to the road-turtles without a huge fuss. And as for Sam, he would say, "God is still working on me with that." Honesty from the hubby; you gotta love it!

I mentioned earlier that part of my childhood took place on my grandparent's farm in West Virginia. Unlike my mom growing up, we had the luxury of both indoor and outdoor plumbing. When visiting my grandparent's farm, I was often tasked with bringing water up from the well-house, a building frame set over natural springs coming off the mountain, just like Mom did as a child. Daily, someone had to bring buckets of water up to the house to be used for extra cleaning, especially if the inside pump was not working properly. Fresh spring water was crystal clear and tasted wonderful.

On occasion we would have murky water because of impurities clogging up the springs; in that case one of my uncles or an aunt would go upstream looking for the culprit. When the problem was located, they would remove it from the stream. Shortly the water was clear again. The origin of the water had not changed, the clean crystal clear product came straight off of the mountain as usual, but it was something that happened in-between it's origination and the destination that caused the mess up. For us, that something is sin.

2. We were created by God and for God, to praise and worship Him. Our purpose has not changed. But with the entrance of sin, the water of our lives has become murky. Only by walking upstream, back to the source of purity can we identify the cause and remove it. When you speak an unkind word, ask the Holy Spirit to reveal its source. Are you willing to walk upstream to remove it? Write down your thoughts:

3. *"Can a fig tree, my brethren, bear olives, or a grapevine bear figs?"* It would go against the nature of the fig and grapevine to produce a totally different fruit. How then can we, as sinners, produce goodness? Explain (**DD -** Find scripture on this subject...)

4. *". . . Thus no spring yields both salt water and fresh."* What does this mean to you?

As you go about your day, choose to walk upstream. Return to the source of pure thinking; refresh yourself in the washing of His word so your choices may reflect the clarity of His love to all who receive a word from you today.

Daily Prayer: *Praise You, O Sustainer of My Days. I fall before You on my knees recognizing You and You alone as the One who has counted the hairs on my head. You know me by name and I stand in awe of You. Strengthen me today that I may walk-the-walk of Your faithful child. Encourage me that I may hear Your words and abide in them. Discipline me, that I may remember You are God and I am not. In Jesus name, Amen.*

Re-Measuring Your Faith-Walk:

Please complete the Faith-Walk Milestone questionnaire and compare it to your first one. How has God grown you during this study?

"I waited patiently for the LORD; And He inclined to me, And heard my cry. He also brought me up out of a horrible pit, Out of the miry clay, And set my feet upon a rock, And established my steps. He has put a new song in my mouth— Praise to our God; Many will see it and fear, And will trust in the LORD" (Psalm 40:1-3 NKJV).

Take a moment and re-rate these statements. Consider how they have changed over the last 5-weeks.

Empty…1…2…3…4…5…6…7…8…9…Full

1. Do I wait *patiently* for the Lord in the following areas?

    Family ____
    Spouse ____
    Work____
    Strangers ____
    Self ____

2. I cry out to my Abba on a *regular* basis. (In joy, sadness, praise, adoration, etc.) ____

3. I experience the Arms-of-God lifting me out of trials *consistently*. (In all things) ____

4. I am planted *firmly* on the rock of faith. (No worry, anxiety, doubt, fear) ____

5. The *Holy Spirit* establishes my steps. (Everything is done His way not mine) ____

6. I sing out a *new song* of praise to God daily. (Fresh-excitement, full of wonder and awe) ____

7. My Faith-Walk *inspires others* to trust the Lord. ____

You have reached the halfway point my sister congratulations! Keep going, you're doing great!

Session 7: Pride: Embracing Wisdom, Releasing Self

"When dealing with people, remember you are not dealing with creatures of logic, but with creatures bristling with prejudice and motivated by pride and vanity."
Dale Carnegie

Session 7: Pride: Embracing Wisdom, Releasing Self

*Weekly Reading: **James 3:13-18 NKJV*** *"Who is wise and understanding among you? Let him show by good conduct that his works are done in the meekness of wisdom. But if you have bitter envy and self-seeking in your hearts, do not boast and lie against the truth. This wisdom does not descend from above, but is earthly, sensual, demonic. For where envy and self-seeking exist, confusion and every evil thing are there. But the wisdom that is from above is first pure, then peaceable, gentle, willing to yield, full of mercy and good fruits, without partiality and without hypocrisy. Now the fruit of righteousness is sown in peace by those who make peace."*

James 4:1-10 "Where do wars and fights come from among you? Do they not come from your desires for pleasure that war in your members? You lust and do not have. You murder and covet and cannot obtain. You fight and war. Yet you do not have because you do not ask. You ask and do not receive, because you ask amiss, that you may spend it on your pleasures. Adulterers and adulteresses! Do you not know that friendship with the world is enmity with God? Whoever therefore wants to be a friend of the world makes himself an enemy of God. Or do you think that the Scripture says in vain, 'The Spirit who dwells in us yearns jealously?' But He gives more grace. Therefore He says: 'God resists the proud, But gives grace to the humble.' Therefore submit to God. Resist the devil and he will flee from you. Draw near to God and He will draw near to you. Cleanse your hands, you sinners; and purify your hearts, you double-minded. Lament and mourn and weep! Let your laughter be turned to mourning and your joy to gloom. Humble yourselves in the sight of the Lord, and He will lift you up."

James 4:11-17 "Do not speak evil of one another, brethren. He who speaks evil of a brother and judges his brother, speaks evil of the law and judges the law. But if you judge the law, you are not a doer of the law but a judge. There is one Lawgiver, who is able to save and to destroy. Who are you to judge another? Come now, you who say, 'Today or tomorrow we will go to such and such a city, spend a year there, buy and sell, and make a profit'; whereas you do not know what will happen tomorrow. For what is your life? It is even a vapor that appears for a little time and then vanishes away. Instead you ought to say, 'If the Lord wills, we shall live and do this or that.' But now you boast in your arrogance. All such boasting is evil. Therefore, to him who knows to do good and does not do it, to him it is sin."

Take a minute and read through these passages of scripture, if you use a different translation, underline where the two translations have different words and phrases of significance. Do any of the differences stand out to you? Why?

    Well my Super-Natural Sister, we have certainly traveled a winding road of transparency these past seven weeks, and I am eager to hear how our Lord has touched your life through this study. In the weeks ahead you will be challenged to dig deeper into your faith-walk. Do you have your spiritual shovel ready?

    Over the course of this study, I introduced the concept of, *Getting Skinny with the Holy Spirit*—an intentional act of drawing our thoughts and actions into alignment with His will in all areas of our lives. Secondly, we discussed our natural state of *Being Fat in the Flesh*—a subconscious act of replaying and displaying negative tapes that keep us believing the lies of the world. By understanding these 2 concepts, we have the option to move into a *supernatural state* of loving who we are because of how God sees us. The next few weeks will require even more transparency on your part. It's about your willingness to peel back the onion, to reveal stinky stuff, tearful stuff, and possibly scary stuff in order to expose the strongholds holding you back from experiencing the positive power of God's truth in your life every day.

> *Reminder, underline or highlight words and write in the margins of your Bible anything that stands out, include the date for future reference...*

Please don't allow your inner *little girl's* fear or the evil one, any opportunity to stop you from completing this incredible journey. Plan ahead for your study time and to attend your weekly meetings. Put more effort into it than you have in the past, and don't lose sight of the goal. If possible; journal every thought that comes to your mind... remember our God is faithful in all things and He has not brought you this far to leave you now. He will carry you when necessary. Your Super-Natural Sisters love you and are praying for you.

Take a minute and list the names of your small group members here. Please pray for God's will, His way, and His timing in an area of life you know they are dealing with.

Over the next three weeks we will look at prosperity, perseverance and taking action. You will be asked some revealing questions; your answers are for your eyes only. If the Spirit leads you, you may ask to share your answers in small group time. Be assured the utmost confidence is to be held by each member with nothing shared outside of your groups. Believing God sees all, hears all, and knows all gives me peace in His selection of your small group members.

This week our scriptures are longer, so we will do things just a bit different. I'm offering you the opportunity to dissect the verses and apply the inductive study habits you have learned over the past six weeks:

1) Extracting God's Truth 2) Personalizing God's Truth 3) Applying God's Truth

I have included PRIDE scripture references in the Resource Charts section in the back of this book. Take time each day this week to ponder some of these scriptures.

Have fun this week! Seriously, this is a great time to consider each scripture, ponder its value, and put into action what God leads you to do.

Be blessed with a heart that is open to the possibilities God has in store.

HUGS (**H**is **U**nfailing **G**race **I**s **S**ufficient). . . Linda

Session 7: Day 1 – Pride: Spiritual Wisdom
James 3:13-18

"Who is wise and understanding among you? Let him show by good conduct that his works are done in the meekness of wisdom. But if you have bitter envy and self-seeking in your hearts, do not boast and lie against the truth. This wisdom does not descend from above, but is earthly, sensual, demonic. For where envy and self-seeking exist, confusion and every evil thing are there. But the wisdom that is from above is first pure, then peaceable, gentle, willing to yield, full of mercy and good fruits, without partiality and without hypocrisy. Now the fruit of righteousness is sown in peace by those who make peace."

1. What truth do these verses reveal? (**DD** - Find scripture on the following subjects. . . meekness, wisdom, good fruits, self-seeking.)

2. What do these verses in James 3 mean to you?

3. How can you apply these verses to your current season in life?

4. Do these verses make you think of a past season or situation in your life? If so, can you recall your age, the circumstances, etc.? You may use short thoughts or sentences below.

Thoughts:

As you go about your day, check your conduct against the plumb line of Christ. Share what you learned.

Daily Prayer: *Praise You Father for You are the giver of wisdom. Have mercy on me as I seek daily to have the mind of Christ in all I do. Forgive me and help me bring glory to Your name in all areas of my life. Amen.*

Session 7: Day 2 – Pride: Earthly Pleasures
James 4:1-3

"Where do wars and fights come from among you? Do they not come from your desires for pleasure that war in your members? You lust and do not have. You murder and covet and cannot obtain. You fight and war. Yet you do not have because you do not ask. You ask and do not receive, because you ask amiss, that you may spend it on your pleasures."

1. What truth do these verses reveal? (**DD** - Find scripture covering. . . envy and bitterness.)

2. What do these verses mean to you?

3. How can you apply these verses to your current season in life?

4. Do these verses make you think of a past season or situation in your life? Why? Explain in using short sentences or phrases to illustrate your age, circumstances, etc.

Thoughts:

As you go about your day, consider the source of your thoughts. Are they from the world or from the Spirit?

Daily Prayer: *Lord, protect my mind. Help me to be alert of thoughts that are not from You. Thank you for loving me, and create in me a heart that loves others in the same way.* Amen.

Here is your mid-week H.U.G. (His **U**nfailing **G**race) from Brenda. . .

At the writing of this, I had just returned from a visit with family, and it struck me how little time we really give to those we love so much. Thinking about them sometimes brings tears to my eyes. It breaks my heart to think that I may never see them again--health, age, an unexpected turn of events could happen. So this time when I traveled home, I made it a point to do or say something Christ-like to each one of them.

We are to minister everywhere we go. To minister simply means to serve. Many question what their ministry is. God has told all of us, even in the meaning of the word itself, that we need to serve others. Jesus gave us a beautiful example of serving in John 13:4-5 when "he got up from the meal, took off his outer clothing, and wrapped a towel around his waist. After that, he poured water into a basin and began to wash his disciples' feet, drying them with the towel that was wrapped around him."

Have you washed any feet lately? I'm speaking in the literal sense as well as in the spiritual realm. God tells us to "love your neighbor as yourself" (Mark 12:31). I know I haven't had any shortage of doing things for me, how about you?

I definitely believe this command includes our families, and yet I often fail to show or speak love into their lives. I'm glad to do "little things" for others. Yet let my husband ask me to get or do something for him and I respond with indignation and hands on hips, "What's your problem? You've got just as much time as I do."

Sometimes, with our families, we refuse to wash feet. Usually, it's because our flesh screams, "Me! I want someone to do something for me."

Of course, we need to continue doing things for others, but we also need to remember loved ones and to honor them with a servant's heart. Jesus took the lowest of positions for us, His Beloved. Shouldn't we be willing to do likewise for our Beloved?

Dear Father,
We come to You with hearts full of love and admiration for You. Please help us to have those same hearts for others. Let us have your kindness, love, joy, peace, and self-control when we approach Your children. Remind us to cherish the family members You have given us and to know that You don't make mistakes in the families You place us. Even in the midst of trials and tribulation, You are there with us to strengthen us, to teach us, to mold us into women of character, women with hearts like Jesus. Let us die to self daily and become witnesses of your grace each day. It is very hard at times, but with You, nothing is impossible. I pray for every woman in this study and ask for Your hand of mercy to be on them. Show them Your desire for every situation they are in and give them wisdom to attain it. We love You and offer praise to You. In Jesus' name, Amen.

Session 7: Day 3 –Pride: Resist the Devil
James 4:4-8

"Adulterers and adulteresses! Do you not know that friendship with the world is enmity with God? Whoever therefore wants to be a friend of the world makes himself an enemy of God. Or do you think that the Scripture says in vain, 'The Spirit who dwells in us yearns jealously?' But He gives more grace. Therefore He says: 'God resists the proud, but gives grace to the humble.' Therefore submit to God. Resist the devil and he will flee from you. Draw near to God and He will draw near to you."

1. What truth do these verses reveal? (Look up scriptures concerning selfishness and confusion.)

2. What do these verses in James 4 mean to you?

3. How can you apply these verses to your current season in life?

4. Do these verses make you think of a past season or situation in your life? If so, how? Explain or document with short sentences or phrases your age, circumstances, event, person, etc.

Thoughts:

As you go about your day, consider the friendships you covet. Is your relationship with Christ number one?

Daily Prayer: *Abba, I know You are a jealous God. You desire my time and praise over all things. Create in me a deeper longing for You, that I may praise You every day of my life. I pray all these things in the name of my savior Jesus Christ. Amen.*

Session 7: Day 4 – Pride: Humble Before God
James 4:9-10

"Lament and mourn and weep! Let your laughter be turned to mourning and your joy to gloom. Humble yourselves in the sight of the Lord, and He will lift you up."

1. What truth do these verses reveal? (**DD** - Find scripture on… Humility.)

2. What do our focus verses mean to you?

3. How can you apply these verses to your current season in life?

4. Do these verses make you think of a past season or situation in your life? Why? Explain in using short sentences or phrases to illustrate your age, circumstances, etc.

Other thoughts:

As you go about your day, seek the pure wisdom that comes from the Holy Spirit concerning humility.

Daily Prayer: *Father God, praise You for You are merciful. Praise You for Your love is without pretense. Thank You, O Lord, for the gift of the Holy Spirit who dwells in me. Fill me to overflowing this day that others may see You through me. I pray this in Jesus name,* Amen.

Session 7: Day 5 – Pride: Judge Not
James 4:11-17

"Do not speak evil of one another, brethren. He who speaks evil of a brother and judges his brother, speaks evil of the law and judges the law. But if you judge the law, you are not a doer of the law but a judge. There is one Lawgiver, who is able to save and to destroy. Who are you to judge another? Come now, you who say, "Today or tomorrow we will go to such and such a city, spend a year there, buy and sell, and make a profit"; whereas you do not know what will happen tomorrow. For what is your life? It is even a vapor that appears for a little time and then vanishes away. Instead you ought to say, "If the Lord wills, we shall live and do this or that." But now you boast in your arrogance. All such boasting is evil. Therefore, to him who knows to do good and does not do it, to him it is sin."

1. What truth do these verses reveal?

2. What do these verses mean to you?

3. How can you apply these verses to your current season in life?

4. Do these verses make you think of a past season or situation in your life? Why? Explain in using short sentences or phrases to illustrate your age, circumstances, etc.

Consider the Cross-References to Price in the Resource Chart section.

As you go about your day, look for opportunities to promote peace. How did you act upon opportunities?

Daily Prayer: *O God, in You alone I find peace. I can become overwhelmed by the world so easily Lord. Help me to rest in Your righteousness, knowing on my own I am helpless. While in You there is always hope. Be with all of our warrior sisters this week, Father. Help each one to rest in You alone. In the mighty name of Jesus,* Amen.

Session 8: Prosperity: Living in a Material World

"Prosperity is only an instrument to be used, not a deity to be worshipped."
Calvin Coolidge

Session 8: Prosperity: Living in a Material World

Weekly Reading: James 5:1-6 *"Come now, you rich, weep and howl for your miseries that are coming upon you! Your riches are corrupted, and your garments are moth-eaten. Your gold and silver are corroded, and their corrosion will be a witness against you and will eat your flesh like fire. You have heaped up treasure in the last days. Indeed the wages of the laborers who mowed your fields, which you kept back by fraud, cry out; and the cries of the reapers have reached the ears of the Lord of Sabaoth. You have lived on the earth in pleasure and luxury; you have fattened your hearts in a day of slaughter. You have condemned, you have murdered the just; he does not resist you."*

Read through the above passage of scripture. If you used a different translation, underline where the two have different words and phrases of significance. Do any of the differences stand out to you? Why?

Reminder, <u>underline</u> or highlight words and write in the margins of your Bible anything that stands out, include the date for future reference.

Take a minute and list the names of your small group members here. Pray for God's will, His way, and His timing in an area of life you know they are encountering. Highlight your accountability sister. . . email her a note of encouragement.

Think about your family members (FM) and loved ones (LO) who need a touch from God in their lives. A touch from God can be prayer for their health, clarity in decisions and relationships, or words of encouragement for any area in which they have a need. Lift them up in prayer and if led to do so (get skinny with the Spirit on this), let your FM's and LO's know you are praying for them.

Be blessed this week with a heart that is open to the possibilities God has in store.

Believing...
HUGS (His **U**nfailing **G**race **I**s **S**ufficient)... Linda

Session 8: Day 1 – Prosperity: Life is Good!
Have you heard of the song *Material Girl* by Madonna? Yeah, I'm dating myself here (you can listen to it online, just Google the name)... Her take, in the song, is if a guy can't come up with the financial means to treat her the way she deserves, then she walks away. The lyrics suggest that she may kiss and hug them but only the ones who have the money will get her full attention.

1. What is your <u>first</u> reaction to the emphasis of this song? Explain.

I was raised in a military family; we traveled a lot, never really accumulating tons of "things" because we would have to move them multiple times in a single year. Okay, wait a minute, is that really the reason we didn't have the newest car, furniture, or fashions? Or is it because we were not in a financial position where *new items* made the priority list? To be honest, that sounds more like it. But still, the constant moving didn't help.

Mind you, I never felt underprivileged or lacking in anyway. Mom and Dad did their best to see to our needs, providing a roof over our heads and balanced meals for our stomachs with the occasional dessert on Saturdays. Talking to Mom and Dad, years later, they would share how disappointing it was not to have given us music lessons or any *extras* that would have made life more fun. Seriously, I never thought about what was missing – for me, life was good.

Life was good, until I moved out on my own and became aware of all the options. You know the things we don't need to survive... but would look totally awesome in our kitchens, bedrooms, bathrooms or backyards. Once I stepped into the world-of-options, my frame of reference changed and I began desiring more than I needed. I can also justify why it's okay. We're told "We need to thrive not merely survive in life." Well, the new things I desired would surely help me to thrive... and that was the mindset I chose to harbor.

At one time not too long ago, I fell into the trap-of-accumulation. I had been invited to a *house* party, you know the kind; invite your friends, everyone buys an item or two, you get something, free as a host, everyone goes on about their way and life is good. Traditionally that's how it works, but on this particular day, a few of the guests came up with an *awesome* idea, "Let's get twelve ladies to host one party a month for a year. We will all attend each other's party and buy a little something. We'll invite other friends, and by the end of the year, we will have received free items for hosting and had a great time of *fellowship*." In theory, it sounded great. In reality – because I never buy a *little* something, I wound up with a closet full —*to the top full* —of items I would never use and a huge depletion of funds in my checking account. Just to be clear, I take full responsibility, no one forced me into this action, it was self-induced. Eventually, I sold some of the items for pennies on the dollar and gave many away as gifts. I still have some in my closet, waiting for the day I have a bigger house with just the right rooms in which to place these beautiful "things." I'm not sure that day is coming anytime soon.

2. What about you? Do you wander through cycles of spending-on-a-whim in your life? Are "Sale" racks calling your name? If so, how does this attitude make you feel?

3. If spending isn't an issue for you, do you have "collectables" of any kind in your home? List them here:

4. If you are not a free-spender, or a COLLECTER OF THINGS, do you horde your finances? What directs your spending?

5. How do you rate your financial stability? (a) Under God's Control (b) Semi-Controlled (c) Out of Control. Explain your answer:

As you go about your day, walk through your home, be aware of what you have accumulated. We will talk about this journey during our *One New Thought* next week.

Daily Prayer: *Abba, be with me today. I desire to see my world through Your eyes. Give me clarity to see where I am focused and what I hold dear as more than "needs" in my home. I praise You for You are my* *strength and my shield. You will keep me from harm as I allow You to guide me day-to-day. Be with me today Father, guide my steps, keep me skinny in You.* Amen.

Session 8: Day 2 – Prosperity: Thy Name is Misery
James 5:1-2

"Come now, you rich, weep and howl for your miseries that are coming upon you! Your riches are corrupted, and your garments are moth-eaten."

1. What truth do these verses reveal about the love of money?

> **Misery**: great unhappiness; source of great unhappiness; poverty

2. Here we find some words of warning to those who are fixated on their own *wealth* (which can be translated to read – anything that takes our focus away from God). Misery is on its way. *"Do not lay up for yourselves treasures on earth, where moth and rust destroy and where thieves break in and steal; but lay up for yourselves treasures in heaven, where neither moth nor rust destroys and where thieves do not break in and steal"* (Matthew 6:19-20). How can having wealth be considered *poverty*?

3. Today's verses are warnings; this means there is hope for change.

Here are a few steps you can take to redirect your desires away from worldly possessions towards the lasting hope in Christ:

- Name the issue you struggle with
- Own the issue—accept that you have a challenge
- Spend "intentional" time with a godly sister for accountability and prayer
- Participate in a structured Bible study to deepen your faith-walk

- MOST IMPORTANT – Spend time in the *word* with the Lord, everyday

4. We spend time with the things we treasure... *"For where your treasure is, there your heart will be also"* (Matthew 6:21). Where are you spending your time?

As you go about your day, thank God for all He has given you. Then ask Him for strength to let some things go.

Daily Prayer: *In You, O God, I find peace. In Your Word, I find refuge. In Your word, I draw closer to You. Give me the desire, Holy Spirit, to want You over all things. In Jesus name I pray.* Amen.

Here is your mid-week H.U.G. (His **U**nfailing **G**race**) from Brenda...**

    Unconditional love is such a foreign concept to most of us. We say, "We love you!" to our spouses, children, family members, friends. But, is the professed love based on our emotions on a given day or in a specific circumstance? My response should be, "Of course not, I do love them always." In reality, I do love them differently based on many factors, mostly my perception of the love they've earned or expressed. Love should not be "works-oriented" or "circumstantial" or even "emotional." And yet, I venture to say that love is conditional in most persons I have known.
    I have studied many scriptures on love, and still I don't believe I have conquered the kind of love Our Lord desires for us to have for Him and for others. I want to. I hope to. I desire to. But, I fall short.
    I know that I can feel great emotion for God when I am having a mountaintop experience. I know I seek God's face when I am in a valley. I also know He loves me even though I can't reciprocate His kind of love in equal proportion. I do love Him, but I still fail to love perfectly. Unconditional love means perfect love. Thankfully, some day, I will love in kind to His love. Until then, I will keep looking to the example we

have of love--Jesus. He is love. "For God so loved the world that He gave His one and only Son, so that whosoever believeth on Him shall not perish but have eternal life" (John 3:16). I will keep reading His Word. I will think on His Word and obey it. I will talk to Him daily. I will allow the Holy Spirit to teach me more about Jesus and transform me into His image one day at a time.

Today, I choose to ponder these divine Words and pray for them to become who I am:

" ' Do not seek revenge or bear a grudge against one of your people, but love your neighbor as yourself. I am the LORD'" (Lev:19:18).

"Love the LORD your God with all your heart and with all your soul and with all your strength" (Deut.6:5).

"And you are to love those who are aliens, for you yourselves were aliens in Egypt" (Deut. 10:19).

"Love the LORD your God and keep his requirements, his decrees, his laws and his commands always" (Deut. 11:1).

"After David had finished talking with Saul, Jonathan became one in spirit with David, and he loved him as himself" (1 Sam. 18:1).

"Let those who love the LORD hate evil, for he guards the lives of his faithful ones and delivers them from the hand of the wicked" (Psalm 97:10).

"Because I love your commands more than gold, more than pure gold. . . " (Psalm 119:127).

Dear Father,
You are Love. You give unconditional love to Your people every day. Let us learn to love one another as You do. Let us love You with a pure heart, not seeking our will, but yours. Let us love You with an all-consuming love. Let us obey Your laws, decrees, commandments and do so with glad hearts. Let us love our enemies and those who do not look or behave as we want. Let us love the unlovely, and remind us that we, too, were once unlovely. Let us grow in our relationships with others, and help us to share You with all who do not know You. Let us proclaim the gift of Your Son to them, so they may have unconditional love and eternal life in You. Draw us to Your Spirit, and let us become more like

Jesus every day. Teach us how to love. In the precious name of Jesus, we pray. Amen.

Session 8: Day 3 – Prosperity: Tempted-to-Accumulate
James 5:3
"Your gold and silver are corroded, and their corrosion will be a witness against you and will eat your flesh like fire. You have heaped up treasure in the last days."

1. What truth does today's verse reveal about our "human" desire to surround ourselves with things that make us feel good?

A few years ago on my radio show *Not Just Talkin' The Talk*, I covered the topic of "clutter". My guest was Kathryn Porter, her book *Too Much Stuff* proved to be a great reference book for me as I began my de-cluttering journey.

In the prologue Kathryn shared "her story." The following excerpt stopped me in my tracks; prompting me to evaluate life and what could happen when individuals seek to find solace in possessions.

"'I am so sorry about your mother. How did it happen?' people asked.

The paramedics had to push aside boxes and bags of junk to clear a path so they could get the stretcher through the house. There was too much stuff.

Boxes, bags, trash, and debris were everywhere, three to four feet high in many places. A narrow pathway carved a trail from the front door to the couch that had become my mother's deathbed. A layer of vomit lined the clutter by the couch.

'Complications of diabetes,' I replied. Yet in my heart I knew collecting too much stuff contributed to her early death. But how do you tell someone your mother was suffocated by a house filled with waist-high clutter?"

This "condition" is now being brought out into the open and is viewed by thousands weekly on *Hoarders*, a reality show.

> **Hoarding:** to collect and store, often secretly, large amounts of things such as food or money for future use.

2. Why do you think people are so drawn to hoarding? Perhaps they grew up in poverty. Is there a deeper meaning than what seems like an easy answer? Do you know anyone who hoards?

". . . their corrosion will be a witness against you and will eat your flesh like fire."

When our dreams and desires are locked up in the earthy ideals and values, we will be destroyed by what we love the most. It will eat away at us, especially if we hang our value on the things of this world. When economic strife comes and it will, some may be devastated, feeling hopeless… to the point of suicide. I pray this is not you. Be assured God did not bring you this far to leave you now. . . He is our faithful Provider. He paid a high price for you out of Love.

3. What are the things you would not want to lose?

4. You can't be sure, but how do you think you would react to bankruptcy?

Even in the end of days, people will choose their "things" over the saving grace of Jesus Christ.

"But the rest of mankind, who were not killed by these plagues, did not repent of the works of their hands, that they should not worship demons, and idols of gold, silver, brass, stone, and wood. . . " (Revelation 9:20 NKJV).

5. *"You who say, "Do not commit adultery," do you commit adultery? You who abhor idols, do you rob temples?"* (Romans 2:22 NKJV) How can individuals who say they despise idolatry still be guilty of it? Idolatry can be defined as excessive admiration or love shown for somebody or something. Explain.

As you go about your day, look around your home; is there something of value you could give away to a friend, family member or stranger? Make a list in the margin of possible gifts to give.

Daily Prayer: *In Your house, O God, there will be mansions, streets of gold, crowns of righteousness... help me to focus on You and eternity, not the things of this world that will pass away. I pray these things in Jesus name,* Amen.

Session 8: Day 4 –Prosperity: Self-Imposed Grief
James 5:4

"Indeed the wages of the laborers who mowed your fields, which you kept back by fraud, cry out; and the cries of the reapers have reached the ears of the Lord of Sabaoth."

Just to give you a little warning, questions **three** and **four** may provoke a peeling back of your *emotional onion*. Pray for the Holy Spirit to guide your thoughts and guard your heart as you proceed.

1. What truth does today's verse reveal about God being ever-present in the lives of His children?

(Look up *Lord of Sabaoth*, who is he?)

2. This week's passage warns those who hold a position over employees or workers to pay them what is due or else face the consequences. The guilt, self-imposed by their actions, will cry in their ears and shout out to the world. In Genesis 4:10, God is speaking to Cain about the death of his brother Able. *"And He said, 'What have you done? The voice of your brother's blood cries out to Me from the ground.'"* Does God show favoritism in hearing the cries of those who are dishonored? Explain your response.

3. We should have a sense of peace, knowing those who wrong us will be held accountable. Why do we continue to worry about them getting their just punishment? Name a situation where you have been wronged:

Does today's verse bring you comfort enough to walk in peace? Explain.

4. If we desire to walk faith-full in every season, we must get skinny with the Spirit, handing over our will for His in everything. When we harbor ill-will or prolonged grief, we are telling God He can't take care of our situation; in turn… we walk away from Him. At some point, we must come back in order to receive His peace in our lives. What would that feeling of peace free you up to do in the following areas?

    Family:

    Work:

    Community:

As you go about your day, breathe in deep the promises of God and say them out loud. He is my ***Refuge*** Psalm 46:1; 62:7. He is my ***Protector*** Psalm 5:1; He is my ***Judge*** Psalm 7:11.

Daily Prayer: *Precious King of Kings, Shield of my Life, protect me from my own desires when they threaten to take me off course from Your will for my life. Make clear my path that I may not be distracted by the evil one. Help me to recognize those things that are not of You, make them glow in my spirit in such a way that I step back immediately. I know full well, Your powers are not of this world, O Lord, and I trust in You with all my heart to guide me in such a way that You receive glory. Amen.*

Session 8: Day 5 – Prosperity: Cursed or Blessed?
James 5:5-6
"You have lived on the earth in pleasure and luxury; you have fattened your hearts in a day of slaughter. You have condemned, you have murdered the just; he does not resist you."

1. What truth does this verse reveal about people who take advantage of those in their service?

     James is not holding back his contempt for the "fat-cats" of society who benefit from the sweat and struggle of others, to the point of living high-on-the-hog, while his workers go home with empty bellies and broken spirits.
     We enjoy watching the *Star Wars* trilogy together as a family every year. In *Star Wars: Return of the Jedi*... the screen opens with a winding dirt road curving around a rocky bend revealing a lone structure just beyond the *Dune Sea of Tatooine*, the mountain palace of gangster and giant slug look-a-like Jabba the Hutt. "*A huge corridor led to the criminal bustle of Jabba's den. In his throne room, Jabba reclined upon a large dais, keeping a sickly eye on the motley horde assembled around him. His every depraved whim was satisfied -- his hunger sated by snacking on live gorgs, his lasciviousness by the performance of his favored dancing girls.*" Jabba is one of the most disgusting visuals I could think of that describes what James is talking about. And yes, I was going for the disgusting... because this kind of evil is repulsive in everyone's book-of-ethics. Though his underlings laughed outwardly going along with any horrible action Jabba might pursue, in the end, they were glad when he was gone.
     Maybe you are more familiar with *The Wizard of OZ*. . . Dorothy, Scarecrow, Lion, Tin Man and, of course, Toto found themselves in the Wicked Witch of the West's castle trying to escape the clutches of her soldiers. In an attempt to douse the flames consuming Scarecrow, Dorothy tossed a bucket of water his direction. The witch was drenched and she melted away, leaving her pointy hat and broom. To Dorothy's amazement, the witch's minions were not mad, they were glad – they handed her the broom and went off boldly singing *Ding Dong, the witch is dead!* No one likes or admires those who hold their position above others, and in the end they get what's coming to them. Do you believe this or does it only work out that way in the movies?

2. What are we to do if we fall under the oppression of a worldly entity? Do we toss water at them in hopes of some "melting action?" Do we plot revenge or 'pray" revenge? Although we may imagine a man-made just response, we are to *be still* and know that God is God.

"But I tell you not to resist an evil person. But whoever slaps you on your right cheek, turn the other to him also. If anyone wants to sue you and take away your tunic, let him have your cloak also. And whoever compels you to go one mile, go with him two. Give to him who asks you, and from him who wants to borrow from you do not turn away. You have heard that it was said, 'You shall love your neighbor and hate your enemy.' But I say to you, love your enemies, bless those who curse you, do good to those who hate you, and pray for those who spitefully use you and persecute you, that you may be sons of your Father in heaven; for He makes His sun rise on the evil and on the good, and sends rain on the just and on the unjust" (Matthew 5:39-45).

3. We are not to resist those who are doing us wrong, even when we have all the evidence in our favor. Slowly peel back another layer of onion, how is this working for you? Can you just walk away? Explain.

    No form of abuse is recognized as acceptable, be it physical or emotional. If you find yourself in this type of situation, seek professional help immediately. Contact one of your study facilitators, and they will guide you to someone who can help.

    Issues of un-forgiveness or bitterness strangle our ability to minister in the fullness of God's power. We must surrender to Him… all issues, believing He alone is enough.

    I believe in the power and privilege of civil disobedience as long as it is done in spiritual righteousness. . . according to God's will. Prayer and petition of the Spirit is a must. Some situations will arise, prompting us to stand up for our beliefs against those in *control of this world*, to walk in boldness knowing God is with us. As we step out in faith on the unseen bridge, He is faithful to provide the brick to make our footing solid. We do not resist in our own strength, we endure to the glory of God.

As you go about your day pray for our government, city and state officials, school officers and community leaders. . . pray in unity, God's will, His way, and His timing.

Daily Prayer: *My strength is in You Lord, my hope is in You Lord, my life is in You Lord, it's in You. It's in You,* Amen.

Session 9:
Perseverance:
Rewarding Persistence!

"Never, never, never give in!"
Winston Churchill

Session 9: Perseverance: Rewarding Persistence!

Weekly Reading: James 5:7-11 NKJV *"Therefore be patient, brethren, <u>until the coming of the Lord</u>. See how the farmer waits for the precious fruit of the earth, waiting patiently for it until it receives the early and latter rain. You also be patient. Establish your hearts, <u>for the coming of the Lord is at hand</u>. Do not grumble against one another, brethren, lest you be condemned. <u>Behold, the Judge is standing at the door!</u> My brethren, take the prophets, who spoke in the name of the Lord, as an example of suffering and patience. Indeed we count them blessed who endure. You have heard of the perseverance of Job and seen the end intended by the Lord—that the Lord is very compassionate and merciful."*

Read through this passage of scripture. If you use a different translation, underline where the two translations have different words and phrases of significance. Do any of the differences stand out to you? Why?

Look at the three underlined segments of the scripture above. Are you encouraged or discouraged by them? Explain.

Take a minute and list the names of your small group members here. Pray for God's will, His way, and His timing in an area of life you know they are encountering with. Highlight your accountability sister… email her a note of encouragement.

Be blessed this week with a heart that is open to the possibilities God has in store.
Believing. . .
HUGS (His Unfailing Grace Is Sufficient). . . Linda

Session 9: Day 1 – Perseverance: Establish Your Heart
James 5:7-8

"Therefore be patient, brethren, until the coming of the Lord. See how the farmer waits for the precious fruit of the earth, waiting patiently for it until it receives the early and latter rain. You also be patient. Establish your hearts, for the coming of the Lord is at hand."

When we see the word "therefore" in scripture, we are to ask, "What is it there for? In this case, James just finished explaining life isn't fair, bad things will happen, and we're all held accountable for our actions towards those in our service or those who "follow" us.

Therefore... we are to be patient.

1. We begin this week with the word patient; let's embrace this with real-life application. Take a minute or two and jot down the names of individuals who are under your leadership (this can be employees, family members, community organization members, etc.). Once that is done, write out next to each name anything that causes you to be impatient, angry, frustrated or out of sorts with him/her. Third, go name by name and ask God to work in you to have patience in each situation.

Therefore... we are to establish our hearts.

2. James says we are to "establish our hearts." What does this phrase mean to you?

Here are a few practical steps you can take to *establish your heart* when dealing with others:

- Consider your motives... Why am I doing this?
- Focus on the Father... Am I giving glory to God?
- Claim God's promises... Am I walking in His truth?

As you go about your day, ask the Lord to bring names to your heart of people who need prayer. Then stop and pray for them. . . on the spot.

Daily Prayer: *Precious Lord, I stand in awe of Your mighty power and Your everlasting love. It is far reaching and life changing. Help me to be a reflection of Your love in my life to those who see me today.* Amen.

Session 9: Day 2 – Perseverance: Do Not Grumble
James 5:9
"Do not grumble against one another, brethren, lest you be condemned. Behold, the Judge is standing at the door!"

> **Grumble**: To complain or mutter in a discontented way; to say something as a complaint.

Therefore. . . we are not to grumble.

1. Do you find yourself grumbling about life? What areas are being revealed to you that need less grumbling? List them here and write out your *concern* about each of them —why are you grumbling?

2. *The Judge is standing at the door,* ready to pass His verdict. Jesus is the Judge not me or you. How can our grumbling cast doubt in the hearts of others?

3. Scripture states, ". . . lest you be condemned" for your acts of grumbling. How do you respond to the ridicule of others?

Brenda Blanchard shared with our initial LMGS small group about a time when a couple of guests joined her *in-home* Bible study. After the prayer requests were shared at the end of their session, the two guests approached Brenda and another study member, Judy, questioning their level of faith. Both Brenda and Judy suffered from debilitating diseases and they were told, "If you had stronger faith, you would be healed."

Closing her eyes to remain focused on God and not on retaliating with pure emotion, Brenda heard these words in her spirit, "Whose faith raised Lazarus from the dead?" She immediately posed the question to the two ladies. They were at a loss for words and quickly excused themselves. You see no person's *faith* raised Lazarus; it was the power of the Holy Spirit through Christ, done to bring glory to God.

Brenda chose not to be intimidated by the ridicule of those two ladies. She got "skinny" with the Holy Spirit and spoke with confidence and truth. We are to walk by faith... believing in God's provision and truth in every situation. Do not buy into the world's counterfeit truths, be defined as *worthy* by the blood of Jesus Christ.

As you go about your day, praise God for sending the Holy Spirit to convict you when you step across the line into discontentment. Ask for His mercy and grace as He reveals deeper areas of struggle.

Daily Prayer: *Father, draw close to me when I struggle; help me to hear Your voice and to feel Your arms of mercy around me. In Jesus name I pray.* Amen.

Here is your mid-week H.U.G. (His Unfailing Grace) from Brenda...

"Ask all the people of the land and the priests, 'When you fasted and mourned in the fifth and seventh months for the past seventy years, was it really for me that you fasted? And when you were eating and drinking were you not just feasting for yourselves?'" (Zechariah 7:5-6).

Why fast? What am I seeking? Ministry growth? Prosperity? Service? Am I seeking God's way, or doing things my way and expecting God to make it happen? Am I asking Him to change circumstances or me?

Recently, the Lord called me to a fast, but not the traditional "no food" kind. In meditating over Zechariah 7 and Isaiah 58, He reminded me that, first and foremost, a fast is a character-building experience.

The Holy Spirit kept pointing me to the closet in my home I dubbed, "The Gift Closet." New knick-knacks, collectibles, and other niceties lined its shelves for future giveaways. Finally, I heard Him. *Give up frivolous shopping. Skip the garage and estate sales, too. Instead, spend time in prayer and writing for me.*

Jesus prayed and fasted for forty days while being tempted. And, He did not fail. Like Him, we have physical, emotional, and spiritual assaults that confront us. Only through prayer and fasting can certain strongholds be rooted out of our lives.

Although curtailing shopping seemed rather drastic, browsing in stores had become like an addiction for me. I had allowed idleness to keep me from God's desire for my life.

My husband seemed particularly happy with this latest revelation. When I asked him if he'd been praying, he laughed and gave a big grin.

Free me, Lord, from the bondage, hindering my growth in you.
Align me to Your heart's desire.
Sanctify me in the truth through Your Word.
Teach me contentment.

In Jesus' name... Amen.

Session 9: Day 3 – Perseverance: Learn By Example
James 5:10
"My brethren, take the prophets, who spoke in the name of the Lord, as an example of suffering and patience."

Therefore... consider the prophets.

1. Look up the prophets Elijah (1 Kings 17-19) and Daniel (Daniel 1, 2, 6, 9) in the Old Testament. What examples can you find of their suffering and patience? List one or two things you learned about each of these prophets below.

Elijah:

Daniel:

2. How can you apply what you learned about the prophets to your current season? How could you use their examples to help others?

3. What *suffering* has God brought you through? Share with your small group if you are led to.

> **Thought to ponder** - God does not prevent us from suffering, but He preserves us in it. Dig deeper, check out 1 Corinthians 10:13.

As you go about your day, consider writing a note of encouragement to a loved one... for no special reason. Then send it... by Snail or E-mail.

Daily Prayer: *Abba, thank You for giving me the examples of the prophets for longsuffering and patience. Prepare my heart for the road ahead, that I may be a living example to others in this season of my life. I pray this in Jesus name. Amen.*

Session 9: Day 4 –Perseverance: Accept the Lord's Mercy
James 5:11
"Indeed we count them blessed who endure. You have heard of the perseverance of Job and seen the end intended by the Lord—that the Lord is very compassionate and merciful."

1. What truth does this verse reveal?

In 1992 at the age of fifty-nine, my mother underwent surgery for a basil- tip aneurism (a ballooning blood vessel between the brain stem and spine). The surgery left her paralyzed on one side. She lost her left peripheral vision, was unable to walk, talk, or care for herself. After nearly fifty years of marriage, this certainly was not the road she or my father had planned to take, but I'm proud to say, it is the one Dad chose to endure for the love of his life.

Dad closed his profitable Real Estate business, remodeled their home to accommodate Mom's wheelchair, and under her close tutoring became a much sought after pie baker, especially during the holiday season. For six years, Dad was Mom's constant companion. He was there when she opened her eyes every morning until see closed them every night. Life was not easy for either of them, but after all, when they married, they didn't sign up for "easy."

"The Lord is very compassionate and merciful." One year after Mom passed away, Dad remarried. Statistics show many widowers pass away shortly after losing the love of their life unless they remarry. My brothers and I are favored by God to have Dad still with us at the age of 82. Indeed, He showed compassion and mercy on our family by providing Elizabeth to come alongside Dad.

In 2012, thirteen years after they married, Dad and Elizabeth stepped into yet another season of life, as they downsized their home and moved years of memories into an assisted living facility. And still, God's provision and mercy remained evident in the love their children have for them and everyone's willingness to come alongside Dad and Elizabeth to make the transition as easy as possible. God is good everyday. He helps us to endure the season's life holds.

> *Endure* in v. 11 (Gk. hupomon) generally indicates inner strength and determination; while *patient* from vv 7, 8, 10(GK. makrothumon) denotes a longsuffering, loving attitude toward others.

2. What are you being asked to 'endure' in this season of life? Have you experienced the mercy of God in it? If so, how?

As you go about your day, breathe in deep the promises of God and say them out loud: He is my Rock from Psalm 18:2; 42:9. He is my Provider from Psalm 78:23-29. He is my Deliverer from Psalm 37-39; 40.

Daily Prayer: *Papa... open my heart so I am receptive to Your mercy. Help me to believe that I am loved and valuable. Organize my thoughts in such a way that when doubt creeps my direction, my mind will recall Your words of truth. In Jesus name.* Amen.

Session 9: Day 5 – Perseverance: Hope In Christ

1. How do you define hope?

Are you confident in God's provision of hope in your current season? Explain.

Look up the following scriptures on hope. Which speaks to you the most right now? Why?

Psalm 16:8-9

Psalm 71:3-5

Romans 5:5

Hebrews 6:17-20

2. We are asked to have patience, to endure, to press onward... in spite of our circumstances. What words of encouragement do you have for your small group sisters in this study to persevere? List your sisters by name with your words of encouragement.

As you go about your day, ask the Lord to strengthen your ability to show mercy to your loved ones and to strangers.

Daily Prayer: *Today, Lord, find me faithful as I desire to see Your hand active in my life. Stir my heart to a state of alertness that You are ever-present in my mind and proven in my actions. Open my eyes to Your purpose for my life as I live each moment for You. In Christ's name I pray,* Amen.

Session 10:
Action:
Putting Feet to
Your Faith!

"Act as if what you do makes a difference. It does."
William James

Session 10: Action: Putting Feet to Your Faith!

Weekly Reading: James 5:12-20 NKJV *"But above all, my brethren, do not swear, either by heaven or by earth or with any other oath. But let your "Yes" be "Yes," and your "No," "No," lest you fall into judgment. Is anyone among you suffering? Let him pray. Is anyone cheerful? Let him sing psalms. Is anyone among you sick? Let him call for the elders of the church, and let them pray over him, anointing him with oil in the name of the Lord. And the prayer of faith will save the sick, and the Lord will raise him up. And if he has committed sins, he will be forgiven. Confess your trespasses to one another, and pray for one another, that you may be healed. The effective, fervent prayer of a righteous man avails much. Elijah was a man with a nature like ours, and he prayed earnestly that it would not rain; and it did not rain on the land for three years and six months. And he prayed again, and the heaven gave rain, and the earth produced its fruit. Brethren, if anyone among you wanders from the truth, and someone turns him back, let him know that he who turns a sinner from the error of his way will save a soul from death and cover a multitude of sins."*

Read through this passage of scripture. If you use a different translation, underline where the two translations have different words and phrases of significance. Do any of the differences stand out to you? Why?

Reminder, underline or highlight words and write in the margins of your Bible anything that stands out, include the date for future reference.

Take a minute and list the names of your small group members here. Pray for God's will, His way, and His timing in an area of life you know they are encountering. Then email her a note of encouragement.

Be blessed this week with a heart that is open to the possibilities God has in store.

Always Believing. . .
H.U.G.S. (His Unfailing Grace Is Sufficient). . . Linda

Session 10: Day 1 – Action: Leaving Footprints of Integrity
James 5:12
"But above all, my brethren, do not swear, either by heaven or by earth or with any other oath. But let your "Yes" be "Yes," and your "No," "No," lest you fall into judgment."

You may not be old enough to remember, but there was a time, not so long ago, when a person's handshake was his/her bond. Everything from selling of cattle to the forming of a corporation was based on a person's *word* "... let your yes be yes and your no be no. . ." A handshake was a sign of his/her integrity.

> **Integrity** - the quality of possessing and steadfastly adhering to high moral principles or professional standards; (completeness) the state of being complete or undivided.

1. Has anyone ever dishonored his or her agreement with you in a business dealing or personal situation? How did you respond to it?

Would you respond differently today? Why or why not?

2. Does your household have integrity "standards" that are non-negotiable? A few examples would be, *we admit when we have done wrong, then move on* or *we take responsibility for our actions.* One more could be. . . *always respect the rights of others.* List yours here:

How are your household standards enforced?

3. Have you considered writing a family *mission statement*? A mission statement is putting down in writing the expectation you have for your family. How will you impact your community? How will you make a positive difference with each other, friends, and even strangers? What does your family want to accomplish in 1 year, 5 years, and 10 years? Ask them and write it out here.

Mission Statement for the _____ Family:

As members of the _____ family, we will make a positive impact in the life of our community, the lives of our friends & strangers, and the lives of our family members.

Family impact on our community is: (Example – To be active members, meet our neighbors, offer a helping hand, invite others to church, etc.)

Family impact on our friends is: (Example – To make them feel welcome in our home, to invite them to family gatherings, get to know them better, to pray for them by name, etc.)

Family impact on strangers is: (Example - To show the love of Christ, to treat them with respect and common courtesy, be sensitive to their needs, etc.)

Family impact on each other is: (Example – To honor one another, use kindness over anger, have weekly family time, be truthful, etc.)

We will accomplish these desires by: (Example – Praying together daily as a family, creating 10 nonnegotiable house rules, attending neighborhood meetings, schedule dinner for friends in our home two times a month, carrying extra food/blankets in our car to give a way to strangers in need, etc.)

As a family we will do our best to accomplish the following:

1-year goals:

5-year goals:

10-year goals:

We agree to be intentional in this mission as a family and as individuals. (List names here)

4. If you were writing your own epitaph (an inscription on a tombstone), what words would reflect your level of integrity?

If you are hard pressed to think of some, ask the Holy Spirit to reveal them. He is faithful to give us wisdom when we ask.

What words come to mind?

Before you head out for the day pray, "Father help me to leave footprints of integrity everywhere I go. And stop me in my tracks when the *prints* I am leaving offend you."

Daily Prayer: *I sing praises to Your name, O Lord, and my heart is on fire with the desire to share Your love with others. Help me to stand taller in Your word than I have ever stood before. Give me the words and boldness to speak them according to Your will, way, and time. Amen.*

Session 10: Day 2 – Action: Casting Lifelines of Encouragement
James 5:13-15
"Is anyone among you suffering? Let him pray. Is anyone cheerful? Let him sing psalms. Is anyone among you sick? Let him call for the elders of the church, and let them pray over him, anointing him with oil in the name of the Lord. And the prayer of faith will save the sick, and the Lord will raise him up. And if he has committed sins, he will be forgiven."

1. Who do you know that is suffering? List names here and pray for them. If you are suffering, ask prayer for yourself as well and include your name in the list.

2. Do you have a friend who is celebrating? List name(s) here and write a note via snail mail or email and share Psalm 92:1-2 *"It is good to give thanks to the LORD, And to sing praises to Your name, O Most High; To declare Your loving kindness in the morning, And Your faithfulness every night. . ."* Sing out the Psalm in celebration with them.

3. Why is it important for the church elders to pray over their sick?

4. How powerful is a prayer of faith? Does the prayer literally heal the sick? Give an example in your response.

As you go about your day, celebrate with, sing for, and pray over your brothers and sisters in Christ in their current season of faith.

Daily Prayer: *Father, I celebrate my relationship with You. As challenges come, guard my heart against the attacks of Satan. Be my stronghold and fortress as I step out boldly in faith to bring You glory and honor.* Amen.

Here is your final mid-week prayer H.U.G. (His Unfailing Grace)

Good morning my supernatural sister… Linda here, I pray our Father has blessed you this week in ways you had not expected. Brenda was gracious to allow me this opportunity to HUG you myself this week. As we fast approach the end of our James journey, I wanted to leave you with a Psalm to contemplate. Psalm 118 covers the endurance of God's love for us; ponder it as you finish our study this week. May this *Truth of Abba* remove any barriers stopping you from seeing how much He truly loves you.

"Give thanks to the LORD, for he is good; his love endures forever. Let Israel say: "His love endures forever." Let the house of Aaron say: "His love endures forever." Let those who fear the LORD say: "<u>His love endures forever.</u>" When hard pressed, I cried to the LORD; he brought me into a spacious place. The LORD is with me; I will not be afraid. What can mere mortals do to me? The LORD is with me; he is my helper. I look in triumph on my enemies. It is better to take refuge in the LORD than to trust in humans. It is better to take refuge in the LORD than to trust in princes. All the nations surrounded me, but in the name of the LORD I cut them down. They surrounded me on every side, but in the name of the LORD I cut them down. They swarmed around me like bees, but they were consumed as quickly as burning thorns; in the name of the LORD I cut them down. I was pushed back and about to fall, but the LORD helped me. The LORD is my strength and my defense; <u>he has become my salvation.</u> Shouts of joy and victory resound in the tents of the righteous: "The LORD's right hand has done mighty things! The LORD's right hand is lifted high; the LORD's right hand has done mighty things!" I will not die but live, and will proclaim what the LORD has done. The LORD has chastened me severely, but he has not given me over to death. Open for me the gates of the righteous; I will enter and give thanks to the LORD. This is the gate of the LORD through which the righteous may enter. I will give you thanks, for you answered me; <u>you have become my salvation.</u> The stone the builders rejected has become the cornerstone; the LORD has done this, and it is marvelous in our eyes. The LORD has done it this very day; let us rejoice today and be glad. LORD, save us! LORD, grant us success! Blessed is he who comes in the name of the LORD. From the house of the LORD we bless you. The LORD is God, and he has made his light shine on us. With boughs in

hand, join in the festal procession up to the horns of the altar. You are my God, and I will praise you; you are my God, and I will exalt you. Give thanks to the LORD, for he is good; <u>his love endures forever</u>."

Precious Father, we adore You from the depth of our souls. Find us this day to be precious in Your sight. Help us to stand tall and strong as beacons of light in the wilderness. Guide our thoughts and keep us safe from the ever-reaching hands of our enemy. Be more real to us this day than You have ever been before and help us to see ourselves as you do. . . righteous, precious, and loved by You because of the sacrifice of Jesus Christ, Your Son. We praise You alone for You are worthy. Amen.

May the glory of the Lord shine down on you this week. May His ways be your ways, and His timing your timing, as you seek His will daily.

Your sister. . . Linda

Session 10: Day 3 – Action: Leading By Example
James 5:16

"Confess your trespasses to one another, and pray for one another, that you may be healed. The effective, fervent prayer of a righteous man avails much."

Today we are looking at prayer as an action step for believers. As we have learned through this study, prayer is not a means to insure that our desires are met; prayer is one way to communicate with God, that we might better cultivate our relationship with Him.

1. How do you react, being told to confess to one another the trespasses of your life?

Do you have a friend you currently confide in? If not, pray for God to reveal someone you might consider and take Brenda's recommendation, "To have a friend, you need to be a friend." (I highly recommend you shy away from confiding in the opposite sex, as this can open doors to inappropriate behavior.)

2. Do you currently pray <u>with</u> your spouse, children, or loved ones?

Do you pray <u>for</u> them? Do they know you pray for them?

If not, how would it impact their life if they knew?

3. *"The effective, fervent prayer of a righteous man avails much."* Would you call your *prayer-life* passionate? Which of the following words describes your passionate prayer-life? Circle those that fit you.

Committed	Scripture-based	Repentant	Intimate
Constant	Worshipful	Reverent	Daily
Closeness with God	Thankful	Filled with Longing	Joyful

List others here:

A great verse to consider concerning your prayer-life is Psalm 42:1 NIV, *"As the deer pants for streams of water, so my soul pants for you, my God."* Does your soul *pant* for God?

4. Knowing that you are blameless in the sight of God because of Jesus Christ, do you pray believing your prayers can avail much? Explain.

As you go about your day, pray for your family members by name.

Daily Prayer: *Abba, increase my faith that I may discover Your perfect will for my life. Increase my faith, that my actions would reflect You in my life every day. Increase my faith that I might be used as an effective prayer warrior. I ask these things in the precious name of Jesus,* Amen.

Session 10: Day 4 –Action: Walking In Confidence
James 5:17-18

"Elijah was a man with a nature like ours, and he prayed earnestly that it would not rain; and it did not rain on the land for three years and six months. And he prayed again, and the heaven gave rain, and the earth produced its fruit."

1. What does *"Elijah was a man with a nature like ours…"* mean? Look up 1 Kings 17-19 the life of Elijah.

How is his life relevant to yours?

2. *"You, however, are not in the realm of the flesh but are in the realm of the Spirit, if indeed the Spirit of God lives in you. And if anyone does not have the Spirit of Christ, they do not belong to Christ. But if Christ is in you, then even though your body is subject to death because of sin, the Spirit gives life because of righteousness. And if the Spirit of him who raised Jesus from the dead is living in you, he who raised Christ from the dead will also give life to your mortal bodies because of his Spirit who lives in you"* (Romans 8:9-11 NIV).

How does this passage give you confidence as you step out boldly to pray?

As you go about your day, look for opportunities to pray with boldness, expecting God to do miracles.

Daily Prayer: *Papa. . . thank you for filling me with the Holy Spirit. You knew life would be tough sometimes, and You love me so much You could never leave me alone, thank you. Help me in times of disbelief that You receive glory in my thoughts, actions and prayers. Amen.*

Session 10: Day 5 – Action: Mentoring With Love
James 5:19-20
"Brethren, if anyone among you wanders from the truth, and someone turns him back, let him know that he who turns a sinner from the error of his way will save a soul from death and cover a multitude of sins."

1. When you share the *Good News* of Jesus Christ, you are planting seeds in the hearts of those who do not know the Lord. When you share how God has worked in your life with brothers and sisters in Christ, you draw them closer to their Lord. Do you understand the power of your testimony? Have you shared your salvation testimony with someone? How did your testimony affect the listener?

Here is mine:

I was raised in a Christian military family where we moved around a lot. At the age of nine, while living in England, I stepped forward in a church service and was baptized along with my older brother. But, at fourteen, during youth camp I finally understood the sacrifice of Christ and gave my life to Him. I'd love to say from that point on my life was always on the straight and narrow path, but I'd be lying. It wasn't until after I had two children, experienced a divorce and suffered through many heartaches that I truly asked Jesus to be the Lord of my life. From that moment on, my walk with Him has been one of joy and peace, especially during the tough times of crisis and disappointment. Yes I still experience heartache, but now I'm not alone, His Unfailing Grace is sufficient.

Write your salvation experience as short or as long as you are led, knowing God will bless it. **(When were you saved? What were the circumstances? Write like you would share casually with non-believers)**:

2. We must understand without a doubt that *we* do not save people only God does that. We are the seed planters and or possibly the ones who water the seed… One way to water the seeds others have planted is to share a life testimony. <u>Read my life testimony below and then write your life testimony.</u> Your Life Testimony is a message of hope, telling what God has done in your life that affirms His love for you. This testimony will help others to know He is real.

Here is mine:

As a divorced Christian mother of two, I was facing one of the darkest times of my life. I was a self-proclaimed failure, grief-filled and feeling totally alone, I entered a time of relational abandonment. I went to bars to dance, drink, and forget… winding up in a deeper sadness than I could imagine. How could God love me after all I had done? But He did and still does. Twenty-eight years later, I'm a happily married mother of four with six precious grandchildren and living a life I never could have imagined. God has given me a community empowerment ministry. He is opening doors for me to speak truth and the ability to write truth to empower lives all over the United States and abroad. God took one lonely broken hearted little girl and gave her a voice to speak His truth to the world. If He can love me and use me to His glory, I know He can do the same for you.

3. Would you be willing to share both of these testimonies if God opened the door of opportunity? Are you feeling any hesitation? Explain how you feel?

As you go about your day, ask the Lord to open the door, or window, and then to empower you to step out to share the *Good News* and His good work in your life.

Daily Prayer: *In You alone do I feel empowered, O God, to step out in boldness. Firm up my testimony that I may be found faithful in Your eyes, O Lord. Bring to my mind godly thoughts that bring forth light causing darkness to flee. Guide me to those whom You have set apart for a time such as this, that my testimony will touch their hearts and quicken their spirit to seek You. In Christ's name,* Amen.

Our 10th Week Faith-Walk Milestone

Take a few minutes and look at your first and sixth week answers to this Faith-Walk measuring tool. Prayerfully consider where you are now after ten weeks of getting to know yourself as God sees you.

Read through the scripture again then take one question at a time, reflecting on the focus word. If you feel you have grown in any area, reflect that in your choice.

"I waited patiently for the LORD; and He inclined to me, and heard my cry. He also brought me up out of a horrible pit, Out of the miry clay, and set my feet upon a rock, and established my steps. He has put a new song in my mouth— Praise to our God; Many will see it and fear, and will trust in the LORD" (Psalm 40:1-3).

Empty...1...2...3...4...5...6...7...8...9...Full

1. Do I wait *patiently* for the Lord in the following areas?

   Family _____
   Spouse _____
   Work_____
   Strangers _____
   Self _____

2. Do I cry out to my Abba on a *regular* basis? (In joy and sadness) _____

3. Do I experience the Arms of God lifting me out of trials *consistently*? (In all things) _____

4. Am I *firmly* planted on the rock of faith? (No worry, anxiety, doubt, fear) _____

5. Is the *Holy Spirit* establishing my steps? (Are things done your way or His way?) _____

6. Do I sing out a *new song* of praise to God? (With freshness, excitement) _____

7. Does my Faith-Walk *inspire others* to trust the Lord? _____

I know the Lord has been working in wonderful ways in your life over the last ten weeks. List a few things that have changed. Be ready to share with the group as the Spirit leads:

Well, my supernatural sister, you made it! You have successfully reached the end of this study on relational transparency based on God's love story in the Book of James.

I pray you have experienced new insight into how your Abba sees you and loves you. I would consider it an honor to hear from you. Please send me an email at linda@lindagoldfarb.com to share how God moved in your life during this study. Also, I'd love to hear your thoughts on the study, too.

If you haven't already, please take a few minutes to visit the www.LindaGoldfarb.com website and sign up for our e-Newsletter to receive monthly words to encourage your faith-walk and empower your relationships, especially with Father.

Most of all I covet your prayer personally. If the Lord brings me or my ministry to your mind, please lift us in prayer according to His will, His way, and in His time. I will do the same for you. Send me an email with your prayer requests.

Be brave, bold, and confident, my sister, as you step out on that unseen bridge-of-faith daily to accomplish all God has in store for you to do on His behalf. He is faithful to equip everyone He calls, and you are called daily to bring glory to Him in all things. Be joyful in the 'being' not the doing, and you will experience Him in a supernatural way.

Blessings and Hugs,

Your sister. . . Linda

Appendix

One New Thought Study Guides

http://www.livepowerfullynow.org/loving-the-me-god-sees

Place the above link in your browser to download your FREE printable Leader's Guide, Prayer Cards, and get access to the free One New Thought videos for this study.

Session 1: One New Thought – Be Willing

Experiencing *growth* and *joy* in times of trials… by the power of the_____ _____.

Be willing to _____ _____ _____ in such a way that others see ____ _____ in us.

Be willing to _____ _____ _____ as _____ to see God at work in our lives.

Be willing to _____ _____ _____ believing in God's _____.

Be willing to _____ _____ above ALL things.

The KEY to growth is finding the strength and wisdom to ____ _____!

Strength… how do you define it? Is it power, knowledge, or physical endurance? Self-achieved virtues of strength are not able to make us willing and truly strengthened in our Faith-Walk. The true source of strength and wisdom is _____ _____.

Words to walk by:

Ps 27:1

Ps 46:1

Is 35:2b-4

Ps 27:14

Worldly Wisdom	Spiritual Wisdom
Sees the message of the Cross as foolishness(1 Cor. 1:18)	Sees the message of the Cross as the power of God. (1 Cor. 1:18)
Does not know God. (1 Cor. 1:21)	Demonstrates the power of God. (1 Cor. 2:5)

Worldly Wisdom	Spiritual Wisdom
Boasts in men. (1 Cor. 3:21)	Glories in the Lord. (1 Cor. 1:31)
Takes pride in human knowledge. (1 Cor. 8:2)	Knows the mind of Christ. (1 Cor. 2:16)
Criticizes leadership. (1 Cor. 4:8)	Submits to spiritual leadership. (1 Cor. 14:37; 16:16)
Relies on the power of words. (1 Cor. 4:20)	Relies on the power of God. (1 Cor. 4:20)
Insists on personal rights. (1 Cor. 8:9)	Becomes a servant of all. (1 Cor. 9:19)
Is insensitive to others. (1 Cor. 8:11)	Edifies others. (1 Cor. 8:1)
Is full of malice. (1 Cor. 14:20)	Walks in the way of love. (1 Cor. 13:1)

Session 2: One New Thought – Breaking the Cycle of Desire/Sin/Death

"Then, when desire has conceived, it gives birth to sin; and sin, when it is full-grown, brings forth death. Do not be deceived, my beloved brethren. Every good gift and every perfect gift is from above, and comes down from the Father of lights, with whom there is no variation or shadow of turning. Of His own will He brought us forth by the word of truth, that we might be a kind of first fruits of His creatures" (James 1:15-18).

See I-Zone Chart in Reference Charts

DESIRE begins ____ _____ _____ .

Romans 12:1-2 says, Be _____ by _____ your _____ .

Philippians 4:8-9 tells us, _____ on _____ _____ .

SIN is _____ to God.

Romans 7:15-20 reminds us, We ____ _____ ___ _____ ____ ___ ___ because of _____ _____ ___ ___ .

Sin can be _____ but is often _____ as something _____ .

DEATH is _____ _____ _____ .

Session 3: One New Thought – Becoming a Reflection of God

How HOT does your life need to get for you to draw closer to God?

Becoming a reflection of God is a process of refinement.

3 Steps found in this week's scripture readings about the refining process…

Step 1 – **Becoming swift to _____.**

John 8:37-47 *"'I know that you are Abraham's descendants, but you seek to kill Me, because My word has no place in you. I speak what I have seen with My Father, and you do what you have seen with your father.' They answered and said to Him, 'Abraham is our father.' Jesus said to them, 'If you were Abraham's children, you would do the works of Abraham. But now you seek to kill Me, a Man who has told you the truth which I heard from God. Abraham did not do this. You do the deeds of your father.' Then they said to Him, 'We were not born of fornication; we have one Father—God.' Jesus said to them, 'If God were your Father, you would love Me, for I proceeded forth and came from God; nor have I come of Myself, but He sent Me. Why do you not understand My speech? Because you are not able to listen to My word. You are of your father the devil, and the desires of your father you want to do. He was a murderer from the beginning, and does not stand in the truth, because there is no truth in him. When he speaks a lie, he speaks from his own resources, for he is a liar and the father of it. But because I tell the truth, you do not believe Me. Which of you convicts Me of sin? And if I tell the truth, why do you not believe Me? He who is of God hears God's words; therefore you do not hear, because you are not of God.'"*

John 8:37 God knows our heart.
John 8:43 Consider whose voice you're listening to.
John 8:45 Do I hear God's voice?

Step 2 – **Becoming slow to _____.**

Eccl 3:7 *"A time to keep silence, and a time to speak..."*

Matthew 10:16-20 *"Behold, I send you out as sheep in the midst of wolves. Therefore be wise as serpents and harmless as doves. But beware of men, for they will deliver you up to councils and scourge you in their synagogues. You will be brought before governors and kings for My sake, as a testimony to them and to the Gentiles. <u>But when they deliver you up, do not worry about how or what you should speak. For it will be given to you in that hour what you should speak; for it is not you who speak, but the Spirit of your Father who speaks in you.</u>"*

Spiritual Hesitation is God saying "I want you to listen."

Step 3 – **Becoming slow to _____.**

2 Corinthians 5:17 NKJV – *"Therefore if any man be in Christ, he is a new creature: old things are passed away; behold, all things are become new."*

Romans 12:2 *"Be transformed by the renewing of your mind."*

Eph. 4:30-32 *"And do not grieve the Holy Spirit of God, by whom you were sealed for the day of redemption. Let all <u>bitterness, wrath, anger, clamor, and evil speaking be put away from you, with all malice</u>. And be kind to one another, tenderhearted, forgiving one another, even as God in Christ forgave you."*

Refinement is not a comfortable process.

Session 4: One New Thought - Love. . . by Way of God's Spirit

Do you consider the *good* being done by non-Christians. . . good?

"If you really fulfill the *royal law* according to scriptures, 'You shall love your neighbor as yourself,' you do well; but if you show partiality, you commit sin, and are convicted by the law as transgressors" (James 2:8-9 NKJV).

How can we as individuals—the church body—fulfill the royal law consistently?

It is _____ _____ the **Royal Law** apart from the **Law of Liberty**.

Royal Law – *Love your neighbor as yourself – even one's enemies*
Law of Liberty – *God's grace & mercy through Jesus Christ*

How can we see others through God's eyes? Only by the power of the _____ _____. When we choose to *get skinny with the Spirit,* we acknowledge His reality, understand His purpose, embrace His plan, and trust His sovereignty. This is a view-point that leads to _____ and _____ living today!

Acknowledge His Reality

The Holy Spirit is _____. He _____ and empowered Jesus, He does the same for _____.

And John bore witness, saying, "<u>I saw the Spirit descending from heaven like a dove, and He remained upon Him</u>. I did not know Him, but He who sent me to baptize with water said to me, 'Upon whom you see the Spirit descending, and remaining on Him, this is He who baptizes with the Holy Spirit.' And I have seen and testified that this is the Son of God" (John 1:32-34 NKJV).

Jesus walked in the _____ to accomplish God's will; we are to do the same. Romans 8:9, 15, says, *"But you are not in the flesh but in the Spirit, if indeed the Spirit of God dwells in you. Now if anyone does not have the Spirit of Christ, he is not His."* and *"For you did not receive a spirit of bondage again to fear, but you received the Spirit of adoption by whom we cry out, 'Abba, Father.'"*

Truth: The Holy Spirit _____ our _____ spirit – so we can walk in Christ's _____.

Understand His Purpose

The Holy Spirit knows what's _____ _____ ____; we must heed His will always, in good times or bad. He knows what will _____ _____ _____; we are to remain skinny in Him…

"Jesus, full of the Holy Spirit, returned from the Jordan and was <u>led by the Spirit in the desert</u>, where for forty days he was tempted by the devil. He ate nothing during those days, and <u>at the end of them he was hungry</u>" (Luke 4:1-2 NIV).

Jesus was _____ _____ the wilderness ____ the Holy Spirit. No surprise; it was part of God's plan. Yet He did not _____. He was merely hungry because the Holy Spirit sustained Him.

Truth: The Holy Spirit _____ _____, so we can _____ _____ as long as needed – albeit 40-days, 3 years or 50 years.

Embrace His Plan

"If you love me, show it by doing what I've told you. I will talk to the Father, and he'll provide you <u>another Friend so that you will always have someone with you</u>. This Friend is the Spirit of Truth. The godless world can't take him in because it doesn't have eyes to see him, doesn't know what to look for. But you know him already because he has been staying with you, and will even be in you!" (John 14:15-17 MSG).

"So I say, live by the Spirit, and you will not gratify the desires of the sinful nature. For the sinful nature desires what is contrary to the Spirit, and <u>the Spirit what is contrary to the sinful nature</u>. They are in conflict with each other, so that you do not do what you want. <u>But if you are led by the Spirit, you are not under law</u>" (Galatians 5:16-18 NIV).

The Holy Spirit is our _____ _____. He will never leave us even though our _____ pulls us from Him. We must lean into Him…get skinny with Him, to hear His words. If we go through the week without connecting with our Power Source, we will be extremely weak!:

Truth: The Holy Spirit _____ _____ us—so we can _____ faith-full.

Trust His Sovereignty

"I am the Vine, you are the branches. When you're joined with me and I with you, the relation intimate and organic, the harvest is sure to be abundant. Separated, you can't produce a thing. Anyone who separates from me is deadwood, gathered up and thrown on the bonfire. But if you make yourselves at home with me and my words are at home in you, you can be sure that whatever you ask will be listened to and acted upon. This is how my Father shows who he is—when you produce grapes, when you mature as my disciples" (John 15:5-8 MSG).

Without Jesus we can do _____!

Truth: The Holy Spirit _____ for us physically and spiritually.

In order to see others as God does, we must rely on the _____ _____ and _____ of the Holy Spirit not the natural spirit we have on our own.

Session 5: One New Thought – Stepping Out on the Unseen Bridge-of-Faith

In life we will be directed by God to step out on an *unseen bridge-of-faith*. Often God directs us into *new territory*, without a roadmap, asking us to simply trust Him. Have you experienced moments like this in your life?

During this week's study, James referenced Abraham and Rehab and their unique *stepping out in faith*. I've listed five areas to consider in their lives and ultimately in your own to see how God has called each of us to His service regardless of background, abilities, or restrictions.

Abraham: Genesis 11:27—25:11 (lived 175yrs)

  Life's Station: A regular man chosen by God to be the Father of all nations... a Patriarch.

  God's Call: A *Lifelong Call* which began with a command. Gen. 12:1-3 Promise made (read list – mighty nation –land of Canaan) Abraham was age 75 and his wife Sarai, later named Sarah, was 65 (mid-life equivalent to our mid 30's – 40's of today). Can we say "mid-life crisis?"

  Sacrifice Required: Uprooting family Gen. 12:1-4; gave best land to nephew Lot Gen 13:8-13; went into enemy territory to save Lot Gen.14:14-16; waited 24 years for – sign of God's covenant Gen.17:1-8; intercedes for Sodom & Gomorrah Gen. 18:23-33; saves- Lot; His ultimate faith walk – sacrifice of Isaac in Gen 22:1-19; and the loss of Sarah (173 years old), Gen. 23:1-2, 19-20.

  Choices Made: Along his journey he—listened to God. . . then lied to men, Went ahead of God, and lied again. . . Abraham proved his humanness yet when the rubber met the road—he was willing to sacrifice his son.

  Action Taken: Believed God & walked in obedience (all the things he did, from leaving his home to offering Isaac as a sacrifice). Was he perfect? No. . . but he was faithful. Hebrews 11:17-19.

Rahab: Joshua 2:1-21

Life's Station: *Intelligent woman*—she was very familiar with Israel's situation (compare Josh. 2:9-11 & Josh. 1:2, 11, 13); *Role model*—she made right decisions and stood firm Josh. 2:4; Gentile Harlot Josh 1:1.

God's Call: *One Act* in her life to help Joshua's spies. . . further God's kingdom.

Sacrifice Required: Possible Death of self and family.

Choices Available: Could have handed spies over to the pursuers/Chose to give sanctuary with expectations of God's provision (oath vs12-13) trusted God—v-21.

Action Taken: Believed in the Israelites' God & hung the scarlet cord in obedience (mentioned in lineage of Messiah—Matthew 1:5 Boaz was her offspring). Was she perfect? No, but she was obedient in her faith—Hebrews 11:31.

Now it's your turn. How would you complete the same areas in your life?

Name: _____ : Date of birth _____

Life's Station: (could be wife, business woman, teacher, mother, doctor, grandmother. . .)

God's Call: *What is God asking of you* in every area of your life? Separate it out if possible – husband – children – parents – community? Consider your passion. . . in your family life, your job, your church, and in your community?

Sacrifice Required: What are some sacrifices you have to make to accomplish this calling?

Choices to be or already made: What are your options?

Action Needed: what steps do you need to take? Consult spouse, wise counsel. . . Hang your scarlet cord?

Are you perfect? Am I perfect? No, but let us be found faithful. . . Matthew 25:21.

Session 6: One New Thought – The Power, Purpose & Promise of Our Faith-Voice

What is our *Faith-Voice*? Our *Faith-Voice* is a _____ _____ of our spiritual-focus when we *speak with intention to glorify God*. To increase our spiritual-focus we look at the power, purpose, and promise of _____ - _____.

1) Faith-Voice Power: Believing that Supernatural Words have power! John 1:1-5 says, "In the beginning was… _____ _____." God created all things by speaking supernaturally.

Genesis 1:3 says, "_____ _____ _____", 6, 9, 11, 14, 20, 22(God blessed them) 24, 26, 28(God blessed them) – God _____ everything into existence. His words are _____ and they have _____.

God created man to have a _____ _____. It is good…for our words to praise God and adore Him. God walked in the garden speaking with Adam and Eve daily. They had an _____ _____.

During Jesus' ministry, *with a word* He – calmed the sea, healed the sick, raised the dead. He supernaturally wiped away our sin. "It is finished!" —This is the _____ _____ of faith-voice power personified. We too can experience faith-voice power daily if we choose to _____ _____ _____.

2) Faith-Voice Purpose: Understanding that *Supernatural Words* have purpose!
"*Do not let any unwholesome talk come out of your mouths, but only what is helpful for building others up according to their needs, that it may benefit those who listen. And do not grieve the Holy Spirit of God, with whom you were sealed for the day of redemption. Get rid of all bitterness, rage and anger, brawling and slander, along with every form of malice*" (Ephesians 4:29-32).

"*Be imitators of God, therefore, as dearly loved children [2]and live a life of love, just as Christ loved us and gave himself up for us as a fragrant offering and sacrifice to God*" (Ephesians 5:1-2 NIV).

When _____ ears give power to _____ words: It affects our thinking —desire – sin – death. Our acceptance of _____, _____, and _____ – is a *cycle* legacies are made of. We see in Genesis 3:1, 4-5, Satan used *corrupt* words to lure Adam and Eve... *accepting* ears gave _____ to his words. The evil one can use the words of others to corrupt us.

Our *voice* can become a _____ _____ to others—Matthew 16:23 says, *"Jesus turned and said to Peter, "Get behind me, Satan! You are a stumbling block to me; you do not have in mind the things of God, but the things of men."*

Roman's 14:13 says, *"Therefore let us stop passing judgment on one another. Instead, make up your mind not to put any stumbling block or obstacle in your brother's way."*

"Be careful, however, that the exercise of your freedom does not become a stumbling block to the weak" (1 Corinthians 8:9).

Redirect common talk into words reflecting our power-filled walk.

Faith-Voice Promise: Trusting *His* Supernatural Word holds promise Philippians 2:8-11 says, *"And being found in appearance as a man, He <u>humbled </u>Himself and became <u>obedient</u> to the point of death, even the death of the cross. Therefore God also has highly exalted Him and given Him the name which is above every name, that at the name of Jesus every knee should bow, of those in heaven, and of those on earth, and of those under the earth, and that <u>every tongue should confess that Jesus Christ is Lord, to the glory of God the Father."</u>*

We know how the book ends! Every tongue will confess... we are to _____ ourselves and become _____ to our Savior & Lord. . . today.

Session 7: One New Thought – Walking Self-Centered or Surrendered?

This week we discovered in order **to sow seeds of righteous wisdom, we must be peaceful in our conduct and thoughts**. Has anyone described you as "peaceful"? What words describe you – _____ – _____ - _____ - _____.

If you are a woman blessed with a peaceful personality, you probably still struggle with issues of envy, self-centeredness and bitterness. Yet… all of us, in our natural self may be lacking in this attitude, we are commanded to do everything in our ability to be obedient to God's word in seeking after a peaceful heart.

It is our_____ to walk _____ _____ or _____… by understanding our _____, we can rewrite our _____… through the power of the _____ _____.

Self-Centered: _____ My _____… _____ is stage _____.

Self is a unique gift from God - Gen 1:26-27. We were created as His _____ _____.

But our actions/choices speak for us at times becoming the source of temptation that leads to the cycle of destruction… desire-sin-death.

Philippians 3:17-19 – *setting our mind* on earthly things… destruction comes.

Matthew 6:24 – no one can serve two masters – choice! Self-centeredness, envy, bitterness are *products of the will.*

Galatians 5:24- The Flesh is *self-focused* with passions and desires

Living in the flesh is our tendency. There is no _____ in a self-centered life.

Surrendered: _____ His _____ … _____ is _____ **stage.**

Surrender is our choice to give someone else position over us... walking under them. How many of you are at ease with that? My natural self, my choleric personality says, "Sure, I'll follow you, if you do things my way."

We must be willing to submit in Love – **Philippians 2:5-11** Christ humbled Himself for us.

Walk in the Spirit to achieve pure wisdom - **Galatians 5:22—26**
_____, _____, _____,
_____ (Patience), _____, _____,
_____, _____, & _____

Surrender must be _____... it will be _____ in our _____ – service to others... planting fruit in others perpetuates the growth in ourselves... fruits of the spirit... which fruit are we lacking? With our family, friends, strangers?

Peace only comes in a _____ _____... His _____, His _____, His _____

Session 8: One New Thought – Cleaning Out the Clutter

Tangible Clutter: Depletes Our Bodies
We _____ physical items out of a _____ _____ of _____, believing what we collect or hold on to will fill an _____ emptiness – in reality it _____ our _____ and _____ our _____ possibilities.

Living Beyond Our Budget – We are _____ to debt —our _____ is lost.
We are _____ by _____ _____.

Questions to ask yourself: Why do I need this? Who does this benefit? What does it represent?

Make your give-a-way list. Assign a name, and give it away now!

Revelation 9:20-21 NIV says, *"The rest of mankind that were not killed by these plagues still did not repent of the work of their hands; they did not stop worshiping demons, and idols of gold, silver, bronze, stone and wood—idols that cannot see or hear or walk. Nor did they repent of their murders, their magic arts, their sexual immorality or their thefts."*

Living Below Our Budget We are _____ from debt —our _____ is gained
We are _____ by_____ _____.

Jeremiah 29:11 says, *"For I know the plans I have for you,' declares the LORD, 'plans to prosper you and not to harm you, plans to give you hope and a future."*

> Active relationships *feed us* better than our need to purchase things ever can!

Emotional Clutter: Depletes Our Relationships
We harbor _____, _____, _____, and _____ from ____ _____ in ways that keep us from moving forward – refusing to _____ ____ and _____ _____, clutters our minds and relational possibilities.

Living in the Past —We are _____ by our _____.

The circumstances of your past are real. They have a true imprint on your life, but they don't define who you are —unless you give them the power to do it.

"Furthermore, since they did not think it worthwhile to retain the knowledge of God, [**They shut their minds to Jesus and no longer valued His teaching**] *he gave them over to a depraved mind, to do what ought not to be done. They have become filled with every kind of wickedness, evil, greed and depravity. They are full of envy, murder, strife, deceit and malice. They are gossips, slanderers, God-haters, insolent, arrogant and boastful; they invent ways of doing evil; they disobey their parents; they are senseless, faithless, heartless, ruthless. Although they know God's righteous decree that those who do such things deserve death, they not only continue to do these very things but also approve of those who practice them"* (Romans 1:28-32 NIV).

Romans 2:4 NLT says, *"Don't you see how wonderfully kind, tolerant, and patient God is with you? Does this mean nothing to you? Can't you see that his kindness is intended to turn you from your sin?"*

For a time, God will tolerate our choices and draw us to repentance.

Living in the Now – We are _____ by _____ _____.
Deuteronomy 34:5-10 NIV *"And Moses the servant of the LORD died there in Moab, as the LORD had said. He buried him in Moab, in the valley opposite Beth Peor, but to this day no one knows where his grave is. Moses was a hundred and twenty years old when he died, yet his eyes were not weak nor his strength gone. The Israelites grieved for Moses in the plains of Moab thirty days, until the time of weeping and mourning was over. Now Joshua son of Nun was filled with the spirit of wisdom because Moses had laid his hands on him. So the Israelites listened to him and did what the LORD had commanded Moses. Since then, no prophet has risen in Israel like Moses, whom the LORD knew face to face."*

1. There is a time to die.
2. There is a time to grieve.
3. There is a time to move forward.
4. There is no pain wasted.

Jeremiah 29:7-15 NIV *"Also, seek the peace and prosperity of the city to which I have carried you into exile. Pray to the LORD for it, because if it prospers, you too will prosper. Yes, this is what the LORD Almighty, the God of Israel, says: 'Do not let the prophets and diviners among you deceive you. Do not listen to the dreams you encourage them to have. They are prophesying lies to you in my name. I have not sent them,' declares the LORD. This is what the LORD says: 'When seventy years are completed for Babylon, I will come to you and fulfill my gracious promise to bring you back to this place. For I know the plans I have for you,' declares the LORD, 'plans to prosper you and not to harm you, plans to give you hope and a future. Then you will call upon me and come and pray to me, and I will listen to you. You will seek me and find me when you seek me with all your heart. I will be found by you,' declares the LORD, 'and will bring you back from captivity. I will gather you from all the nations and places where I have banished you,' declares the LORD, 'and will bring you back to the place from which I carried you into exile."*

God desires each of us to be His – _____, _____, and _____. It takes complete _____. The release of physical items, emotional baggage, and spiritual discontent is the only way to truly reach the point of *Aha* in our relationship with God. When the clutter of the world is removed, we have a sense of well being, contentment, and peace. We are able to walk faith-full in every season of life.

Check out these websites for more information covered in this One New Thought.

www.JillSwanson.com – Image Specialist
www.DaveRamsey.com – Financial Specialist

Session 9: One New Thought – Embracing H.O.P.E.

Perseverance can be an overwhelming word. Let's look at four embraceable actions of HOPE.

Honor His way... God's _____ is _____ and if we desire to walk *faith-full* we must honor God's "way." At the end of his letter to the Philippians, Paul takes a deep breath in chapter 4 verse 8 and says, "Finally..." meaning, after all that's been said and done, after everything I have shared with you – here is my last thought – his *One New Thought*. . . on living life God's way.

*"Finally, brethren, **whatever is** true, **whatever is** honorable, **whatever is** right, **whatever is** pure, **whatever is** lovely, **whatever is** of good repute, if there **is** any excellence and if anything worthy of praise, **dwell on these things**"* (Philippians 4:8 ESV). This puts a whole new slant on the "whatever's" in life, doesn't it?

In order to _____, we must have a _____ _____. This is a great day-in day-out practice.

In addition to a focal point for daily living, we need to remember God's will for us as found in Romans 8:28, *"And we know that **in all things God works for the good of those who love him**, who have been called **according to his purpose**."*

Who is this verse talking about when it says, "those who love Him?" It is those who believe in Jesus as their Lord and Savior.

How can we honor God's way? We need to be _____ to His _____.

Open to **O**bey His will. . . It begins and ends with _____ _____, in our _____ and in our _____.

"Jesus responded, 'Who do you think are my mother and brothers?' Looking around, taking in everyone seated around him, he said, 'Right here, right in front of you—my mother and my brothers. Obedience is thicker than blood. **The person who obeys God's will** is my brother and sister and mother'" (Mark 3:33 MSG).

"**If anyone chooses to do God's will**, he will find out whether my teaching comes from God or whether I speak on my own" (John 7:17 NIV)

"And he who searches our hearts knows the mind of the Spirit, because **the Spirit intercedes for the saints in accordance with God's will**" (Romans 8:27 NIV).

God knows our hearts. The Spirit intercedes on our behalf according to God's will, so it only makes sense to be open to it. . . right?

Let's recap, **H** – we are to *honor* God's way, **O** - we are *open* to obey His will, then what? We wait!

Even when physical pain, broken relationships and financial devastation comes… we wait and we often wonder, "God, are you there?"
The good news is, yes He is here. He has been from the beginning of time, for His timing is perfect and we are _____ in His _____.

Perfected in His time… Paul didn't volunteer for his service to God nor was he, appointed to it by a committee. He was chosen by God Himself according to His way and will. We, too, are _____ by God for a _____ _____ _____ as seen in Ephesians 1:3-10.

"Praise be to the God and Father of our Lord Jesus Christ, who has blessed us in the heavenly realms with every spiritual blessing in Christ. For **he chose us in him before the creation of the world** *to be holy and blameless in his sight. In love he predestined us to be adopted as his sons through Jesus Christ, in accordance with his pleasure and will— to the praise of his glorious grace, which he has freely given us in the One he loves. In him we have redemption through his blood, the forgiveness of sins, in accordance with the riches of God's grace that he lavished on us with all wisdom and understanding. And he made known to us the mystery of his will according to his good pleasure, which he purposed in Christ,* **to be put into effect when the times will have reached their fulfillment**—*to bring all things in heaven and on earth together under one head, even Christ"* (Ephesians 1:3-10 NIV).

So if we are not given specifics as to ". . .**when the times will have reached their fulfillment**" are we to sit and sulk? Or, are we to take one day at a time. . . every season for it's worth and value, stepping out and believing He will guide and direct us according to His way, will and time?

If we are to embrace hope, the answer is yes... so where does the strength come from to make it day-to-day not knowing God's timing? We are _____ by His _____.

Empowered by His word. . . We are told it's not the amount of time we spend with our children or loved ones that counts, but the quality of that time. In reference to time spent with the Lord, the amount of time and even quality is trumped by the frequency. <u>Empowerment comes through daily portions</u>, not weekly or semi-annually stuffing of the word—or even through organized studies or events.

We are not to fast when it comes to God's word.

Jesus was empowered by speaking God's word back to Satan during His 40-days in the desert. Though His body fasted, His spirit was renewed by His testimony.

"And the devil said to Him, 'If You are the Son of God, command this stone to become bread.' **But Jesus answered him, saying, 'It is written, 'Man shall not live by bread alone, but by every word of God.'**... And the devil said to Him, 'All this authority I will give You, and their glory; for *this* has been delivered to me, and I give it to whomever I wish. Therefore, if You will worship before me, all will be Yours.' **And Jesus answered and said to him, 'Get behind Me, Satan! For it is written, 'You shall worship the LORD your God, and Him only you shall serve.'"** Then he brought Him to Jerusalem, set Him on the pinnacle of the temple, and said to Him, 'If You are the Son of God, throw Yourself down from here. For it is written: *'He shall give His angels charge over you, To keep you,'* and, *'In their hands they shall bear you up, Lest you dash your foot against a stone."* **And Jesus answered and said to him, 'It has been said, 'You shall not tempt the LORD your God.'"** Now when the devil had ended every temptation, he departed from Him until an opportune time" (Luke 4:1-13 NKJV).

Jesus proved He was a great student of scripture. He could recall it at any time, so it goes without saying, spending time in God's word, is time well spent.

If Christ used God's word as His protection in the desert, doesn't it make sense to follow His lead? He is our _____ _____ _____.

God desires His children to _____. He loves to bless us according to His will and His way. As we endure the _____ _____ _____ and press onward, in His _____.

His timing is made perfect in our lives. I pray you will embrace these renewed actions of hope as you step forward in your faith-walk.

Session 10: One New Thought – Growing Pro-Active Relationships

Lordship: My God Relationship Schedule a daily personal time with the Lord, write it, log it, journal it. This is a *high priority* step of obedience to the Lord.

What Time of day works best for you?

What Location allows you a peaceful setting?

As a personal-influencer in your home, encourage, don't demand, other family members to begin their personal time with God.

Legacy: My Family Relationship Find a scripture verse that speaks to your *purpose* as a Family of the Most High God. See 'I Am' chart. Write it out, memorize it, say it out loud daily for the next two-weeks.

Revelation 12:11 reads, *"They overcame him [Satan] by the blood of the Lamb and the word of their testimony. . ."* Understanding the power of our testimony, ask each family member to write out his/her personal salvation testimony and life testimony. Check out tips on writing your testimony at:

http://christianity.about.com/od/testimonies/a/howtotestimony.htm

Singles, Couples, and Parents write out your "family mission statement." For children who are not at the age-of-accountability, parents can write out a *word* of encouragement for their lives.

_____ -

_____ -

_____ -

Leadership: My Community Relationship ... Mentoring and investing in the lives of others is where God is seen in us and through us by everyday people. List three areas of service available in your community, then follow up by finding out how you can get involved.

Opportunity 1 –

Opportunity 2 –

Opportunity 3 –

Resource Charts

Outside Stimulus Influences our I-Zone

⇩

Perception leads to Sensory Memory

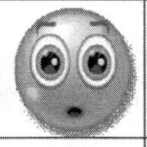

⇩

| TOUCH | SEE | HEAR | TASTE | SMELL |

⇩

Attention leads to Short-Term Memory

⇩

Repetition leads to Long-Term Memory

⇩

No Delete Button in the Brain
Re-thinking is needed to remove old messages!

Cross-References to James 4:11-17
(New American Standard version)

Referencing James 4:11 - *"¹¹ Do not speak evil of one another, brethren. He who speaks evil of a brother and judges his brother, speaks evil of the law and judges the law. But if you judge the law, you are not a doer of the law but a judge."*

2 Cor 12:20 - "For I am afraid that perhaps when I come I may find you to be not what I wish and may be found by you to be not what you wish; that perhaps there will be strife, jealousy, angry tempers, disputes, slanders, gossip, arrogance, disturbances."

James 5:9 - "Do not complain, brethren, against one another, so that you yourselves may not be judged; behold, the Judge is standing right at the door."

1 Peter 2:1 - "Therefore, putting aside all malice and all deceit and hypocrisy and envy and all slander"

James 5:7 - "Therefore be patient, brethren, until the coming of the Lord The farmer waits for the precious produce of the soil, being patient about it, until it gets the early and late rains."

Romans 14:4 - "Who are you to judge the servant of another? To his own master he stands or falls; and he will stand, for the Lord is able to make him stand."

James 2:8 - "If, however, you are fulfilling the royal law according to the Scripture, "YOU SHALL LOVE YOUR NEIGHBOR AS YOURSELF," you are doing well."

James 1:22 - "But prove yourselves doers of the word, and not merely hearers who delude themselves."

Cross reference for James 4:12 - *"There is one Lawgiver, who is able to save and to destroy. Who are you to judge another?"*

Isaiah 33:22 - "For the LORD is our judge, The LORD is our lawgiver, The LORD is our king; He will save us."

Matthew 10:28 - "Do not fear those who kill the body but are unable to kill the soul; but rather fear Him who is able to destroy both soul and body in hell."

Cross reference James 4:13 – *"Come now, you who say, "Today or tomorrow we will go to such and such a city, spend a year there, buy and sell, and make a profit"*

James 5:1 - "Come now, you rich, weep and howl for your miseries which are coming upon you."

Proverbs 27:1 - "Do not boast about tomorrow, For you do not know what a day may bring forth."

Luke 12:18-20 - "Then he said, 'This is what I will do: I will tear down my barns and build larger ones, and there I will store all my grain and my goods. 'And I will say to my soul, "Soul, you have many goods laid up for many years to come; take your ease, eat, drink and be merry."' "But God said to him, 'You fool! This very night your soul is required of you; and now who will own what you have prepared?'"

Cross reference James 4:14 *"whereas you do not know what will happen tomorrow. For what is your life? It is even a vapor that appears for a little time and then vanishes away."*

Job 7:7 - "Remember that my life is but breath; My eye will not again see good."

Psalm 39:5 - "Behold, You have made my days as handbreadths, And my lifetime as nothing in Your sight; Surely every man at his best is a mere breath. Selah."

Psalm 102:3 - "For my days have been consumed in smoke, And my bones have been scorched like a hearth."

Psalm 144:4 - "Man is like a mere breath; His days are like a passing shadow."

Cross reference James 4:15 - *"Instead you ought to say, "If the Lord wills, we shall live and do this or that."*

Acts 18:21 - "but taking leave of them and saying, "I will return to you again if God wills," he set sail from Ephesus."

Cross reference James 4:16 – *"But now you boast in your arrogance. All such boasting is evil."*

1 Corinthians 5:6 - "Your boasting is not good Do you not know that a little leaven leavens the whole lump of dough?"

Cross reference James 4:17 - *"Therefore, to him who knows to do good and does not do it, to him it is sin."*

Luke 12:47 - "And that slave who knew his master's will and did not get ready or act in accord with his will, will receive many lashes."

John 9:41 - "Jesus said to them, "If you were blind, you would have no sin; but since you say, 'We see,' your sin remains."

2 Peter 2:21 - "For it would be better for them not to have known the way of righteousness, than having known it, to turn away from the holy commandment handed on to them."

PRIDE References

2 CHRONICLES 26:16

New International Version:

- But after Uzziah became powerful, his **pride** led to his downfall. He was unfaithful to the LORD his God, and entered the temple of the LORD to burn incense on the altar of incense (2 Chronicles 26:15-17 (in Context) 2 Chronicles 26 (Whole Chapter)).

- [*The Penalty for Uzziah's **Pride***] But when he was strong his heart was lifted up, to his destruction, for he transgressed against the LORD his God by entering the temple of the LORD to burn incense on the altar of incense (2 Chronicles 26:15-17 (in Context) 2 Chronicles 26 (Whole Chapter)).

2 CHRONICLES 32:26
New International Version

- Then Hezekiah repented of the **pride** of his heart, as did the people of Jerusalem; therefore the LORD's wrath did not come upon them during the days of Hezekiah (2 Chronicles 32:25-27 (in Context) 2 Chronicles 32 (Whole Chapter))

New King James Version

- Then Hezekiah humbled himself for the **pride** of his heart, he and the inhabitants of Jerusalem, so that the wrath of the LORD did not come upon them in the days of Hezekiah (2 Chronicles 32:25-27 (in Context) 2 Chronicles 32 (Whole Chapter))

PSALM 10:2
New American Standard Bible

- In **pride** the wicked hotly pursue the afflicted;Let them be caught in the plots which they have devised (Psalm 10:1-3 (in Context) Psalm 10 (Whole Chapter)).

New King James Version

- The wicked in his **pride** persecutes the poor;Let them be caught in the plots which they have devised (Psalm 10:1-3 (in Context) Psalm 10 (Whole Chapter)).

PSALM 10:4

New International Version

- In his **pride** the wicked does not seek him; in all his thoughts there is no room for God (Psalm 10:3-5 (in Context) Psalm 10 (Whole Chapter)).

English Standard Version

- In the **pride** of his face the wicked does not seek him; all his thoughts are, "There is no God." (Psalm 10:3-5 (in Context) Psalm 10 (Whole Chapter).

PSALM 59:12

New International Version

- For the sins of their mouths, for the words of their lips, let them be caught in their **pride**. For the curses and lies they utter (Psalm 59:11-13 (in Context) Psalm 59 (Whole Chapter)).

New King James Version

- For the sin of their mouth and the words of their lips,Let them even be taken in their **pride**, And for the cursing and lying which they speak (Psalm 59:11-13 (in Context) Psalm 59 (Whole Chapter)).

PROVERBS 8:13

New International Version

- To fear the LORD is to hate evil; I hate **pride** and arrogance, evil behavior and perverse speech (Proverbs 8:12-14 (in Context) Proverbs 8 (Whole Chapter)).

New King James Version

- The fear of the LORD is to hate evil; **Pride** and arrogance and the evil way And the perverse mouth I hate (Proverbs 8:12-14 (in Context) Proverbs 8 (Whole Chapter)).

PROVERBS 11:2

New International Version

- When **pride** comes, then comes disgrace, but with humility comes wisdom (Proverbs 11:1-3 (in Context) Proverbs 11 (Whole Chapter)).

New King James Version

- When **pride** comes, then comes shame; But with the humble is wisdom (Proverbs 11:1-3 (in Context) Proverbs 11 (Whole Chapter)).

PROVERBS 16:18

New International Version

- **Pride** goes before destruction, a haughty spirit before a fall (Proverbs 16:17-19 (in Context) Proverbs 16 (Whole Chapter)).

New King James Version

- **Pride** goes before destruction, And a haughty spirit before a fall (Proverbs 16:17-19 (in Context) Proverbs 16 (Whole Chapter)).

PROVERBS 29:23

New International Version

- A man's **pride** brings him low, but a man of lowly spirit gains honor (Proverbs 29:22-24 (in Context) Proverbs 29 (Whole Chapter)).

New King James Version

- A man's **pride** will bring him low, But the humble in spirit will retain honor (Proverbs 29:22-24 (in Context) Proverbs 29 (Whole Chapter)).

The Message

- **Pride** lands you flat on your face; humility prepares you for honors (Proverbs 29:22-24 (in Context) Proverbs 29 (Whole Chapter)).

ISAIAH 2:17

New International Version

- The arrogance of man will be brought low and the **pride** of men humbled; the LORD alone will be exalted in that day (Isaiah 2:16-18 (in Context) Isaiah 2 (Whole Chapter)).

ISAIAH 16:6

New International Version

- We have heard of Moab's **pride**— her overweening **pride** and conceit, her **pride** and her insolence— but her boasts are empty (Isaiah 16:5-7 (in Context) Isaiah 16 (Whole Chapter)).

New King James Version

- We have heard of the **pride** of Moab— He is very proud— Of his haughtiness and his **pride** and his wrath; But his lies shall not be so (Isaiah 16:5-7 (in Context) Isaiah 16 (Whole Chapter)).

ISAIAH 23:9

New International Version

- The LORD Almighty planned it, to bring low the **pride** of all glory and to humble all who are renowned on the earth (Isaiah 23:8-10 (in Context) Isaiah 23 (Whole Chapter)).

New King James Version

- The LORD of hosts has purposed it, To bring to dishonor the **pride** of all glory, To bring into contempt all the honorable of the earth (Isaiah 23:8-10 (in Context) Isaiah 23 (Whole Chapter)).

JEREMIAH 13:17

New International Version

- But if you do not listen, I will weep in secret because of your **pride**; my eyes will weep bitterly, overflowing with tears, because the LORD's flock will be taken captive (Jeremiah 13:16-18 (in Context) Jeremiah 13 (Whole Chapter)).

New King James Version

- But if you will not hear it, My soul will weep in secret for your **pride**; My eyes will weep bitterly And run down with tears, Because the LORD's flock has been taken captive (Jeremiah 13:16-18 (in Context) Jeremiah 13 (Whole Chapter)).

JEREMIAH 49:16

New International Version

- The terror you inspire and the **pride** of your heart have deceived you, you who live in the clefts of the rocks, who occupy the heights of the hill. Though you build your nest as high as the eagle's, from there I will bring you down," declares the LORD (Jeremiah 49:15-17 (in Context) Jeremiah 49 (Whole Chapter)).

New King James Version

- Your fierceness has deceived you, The **pride** of your heart, O you who dwell in the clefts of the rock, Who hold the height of the hill!

Though you make your nest as high as the eagle, I will bring you down from there," says the LORD (Jeremiah 49:15-17 (in Context) Jeremiah 49 (Whole Chapter)).

MARK 7:22

New King James Version

- thefts, covetousness, wickedness, deceit, lewdness, an evil eye, blasphemy, **pride**, foolishness (Mark 7:21-23 (in Context) Mark 7 (Whole Chapter)).

ROMANS 12:4

The Message

- In this way we are like the various parts of a human body. Each part gets its meaning from the body as a whole, not the other way around. The body we're talking about is Christ's body of chosen people. Each of us finds our meaning and function as a part of his body. But as a chopped-off finger or cut-off toe we wouldn't amount to much, would we? So since we find ourselves fashioned into all these excellently formed and marvelously functioning parts in Christ's body, let's just go ahead and be what we were made to be, without enviously or **pride**fully comparing ourselves with each other, or trying to be something we aren't (Romans 12:3-5 (in Context) Romans 12 (Whole Chapter)).

1 JOHN 2:16

English Standard Version

- For all that is in the world— the desires of the flesh and the desires of the eyes and **pride** in possessions—is not from the Father but is from the world (1 John 2:15-17 (in Context) 1 John 2 (Whole Chapter)).

New King James Version

- For all that is in the world—the lust of the flesh, the lust of the eyes, and the **pride** of life—is not of the Father but is of the world.

I Am... My Identity in Christ

I am... adopted by God	"God decided in advance to adopt us into his own family by bringing us to himself through Jesus Christ. This is what he wanted to do, and it gave him great pleasure." Eph. 1:5 NLT
I am... justified	"Therefore, since we have been made right in God's sight by faith, we have peace with God because of what Jesus Christ our Lord has done for us." Romans 5:1 NLT
I am... sanctified	"Some of you were once like that. But you were cleansed; <u>you were made holy</u>; you were made right with God by calling on the name of the Lord Jesus Christ and by the Spirit of our God." 1 Corinthians 6:11 NLT
I am... redeemed	"In him we have redemption through his blood, the forgiveness of sins, in accordance with the riches of God's grace." Ephesians 1:7 NIV
I am... reconciled to God	"For if, when we were God's enemies, we were reconciled to Him through the death of his Son, how much more, having been reconciled, shall we be saved through his life!" Romans 5:10 NIV
I am... a child of God	"If we confess our sins, he is faithful and just and will forgive us Our sins and purify us from all unrighteousness." 1 John 1:9 NIV
I am... an ambassador for Christ	"We are therefore Christ's ambassadors, as though God were making his appeal through us. We implore you on Christ's behalf: Be reconciled to God. " 2 Corinthians 5:20 NIV
I am... called to God's purpose	"And we know that in all things God works for the good of those who love him, who have been called according to his purpose." Romans 8:28 NIV

Terms of Theology

Here are some basic terms from theology to keep handy as we proceed through the study. I thought they would be helpful for this time in our journey... Linda

Faith: Complete trust in and commitment to God.
"² Watch out for those dogs, those people who do evil, those mutilators who say you must be circumcised to be saved. ³ For we who worship by the Spirit of God are the ones who are truly circumcised. We rely on what Christ Jesus has done for us. We put no confidence in human effort, ⁴ though I could have confidence in my own effort if anyone could. Indeed, if others have reason for confidence in their own efforts, I have even more! ⁵ I was circumcised when I was eight days old. I am a pure-blooded citizen of Israel and a member of the tribe of Benjamin—a real Hebrew if there ever was one! I was a member of the Pharisees, who demand the strictest obedience to the Jewish law. ⁶ I was so zealous that I harshly persecuted the church. And as for righteousness, I obeyed the law without fault. ⁷ I once thought these things were valuable, but now I consider them worthless because of what Christ has done. ⁸ Yes, everything else is worthless when compared with the infinite value of knowing Christ Jesus my Lord. For his sake I have discarded everything else, counting it all as garbage, so that I could gain Christ ⁹ and become one with him. I no longer count on my own righteousness through obeying the law; rather, I become righteous through faith in Christ. For God's way of making us right with himself depends on faith" (Philippians 3:2-9 NLT).

Grace: Undeserved acceptance and love from God.
"⁸ For by grace you have been saved through faith, and that not of yourselves; it is the gift of God. . ." (Ephesians 2:8 NKJV).

Salvation: Deliverance from the power and penalty of sin.
⁸ For by grace you have been saved through faith, and that not of yourselves; it is the gift of God. . . " (Ephesians 2:8 NKJV).

Justification: First act of salvation – being brought into a right relationship with God through Jesus Christ.

"But now a righteousness from God, apart from law, has been made known, to which the Law and the Prophets testify. This righteousness from God comes through faith in Jesus Christ to all who believe. There is no difference, for all have sinned and fall short of the glory of God, and are justified freely by his grace through the redemption that came by Christ Jesus. God presented him as a sacrifice of atonement, through faith in his blood. He did this to demonstrate his justice, because in his forbearance he had left the sins committed beforehand unpunished— he did it to demonstrate his justice at the present time, so as to be

just and the one who justifies those who have faith in Jesus" (Romans 3:21-26 NIV).

Sanctification: A process in which the Holy Spirit works in the life of a believer resulting in increasing personal holiness and a close relationship with God.

"But we are bound to give thanks to God always for you, brethren beloved by the Lord, because God from the beginning chose you for salvation through sanctification by the Spirit and belief in the truth. . . " (2 Thessalonians 2:13 NKJV).

Glorification: Last act of salvation when a believer is transformed into the likeness of Jesus Christ.

"And having chosen them, he called them to come to him. And having called them, he gave them right standing with himself. And having given them right standing, he gave them his glory" (Romans 8:30).

I'd love to hear your thoughts on this study, email me at:
linda@lindagoldfarb.com

Here is just a taste of other topics I speak and write on. . .

The Power of Positive
...overcoming "She" fears that shut us down

Linda repositions the Mirror-of-Lies so women can embrace the "she" God sees, exposing the lies we believe.
interactive
90 minute session
For Women and Teens

The Power of Sisterhood!
...standing in the gap!

By connecting at root-level, women can impact our community in a great way… Linda teaches us to stand in the gap as Mentors, Encouragers, and Spiritual Sisters.
60-90 minute session

A Redwood Tree lesson!

Live… Laugh… Love…
The ABC's to a Joy-Filled Life

Linda empowers your community to live a Joy-Filled life everyday in this interactive
90 minute session

For
Men and Women

Diamonds in the Rough-Stuff
...discovering how to shine in spite of life!

Women love diamonds but we don't see ourselves as one. This session reveals the multifaceted sides of a woman and how God makes us shine in spite of our stuff.
60-90 minute session

Ladies Favorite!

You are invited to join us online at www.LindaGoldfarb.com where we offer free resources to empower your walk every day!

NOTES

NOTES

NOTES

Made in the USA
San Bernardino, CA
26 March 2015